The Quantum Leap Coach System

A Streamlined Approach To Extraordinary Results In Coaching

Femke Mortimore MSc.

The Coach Mentor

Reno, Nevada

The Coach Mentor
1890 Daniel Webster Drive
Reno, NV 89509
www.thecoachmentor.org

Ordering Information:
Quantity sales. Special discounts are available on quantity purchases by corporations, associations, and others. For details, contact the "Special Sales Department" at the address above.

The Quantum Leap Coach System/ Femke Mortimore. -- 1st ed.
ISBN 978-0-9996848-1-8

Illustrations by Sanyukta Stargazer

Visit The Coach Mentor online at https://www.thecoachmentor.org

Workbook

This book comes with a free online toolkit. You can find it right here:
https://www.thecoachmentor.org/ql-toolkit

Dedication to Finnegan

Everything should be made as simple as possible, but not simpler.

—Albert Einstein

Contents

Preface

MY TODDLER SON USUALLY sits between my husband and I for dinner. He is learning how to use a fork and every time he manages to pick up a piece of food and bring it to his mouth, he claps. Then he looks at me and his daddy, and waits for us to clap along with him. He has that feeling all the time. He's recently learnt how to say 'car', so whenever a car or truck comes by he'll say it. He says it in the sweetest voice ever: "Car." And then he claps. He used to clap for drinking water out of a cup or going down a step without holding on to something. It seems that once it becomes normal, he stops clapping. There are new things to clap for.

Accomplishment. It's a great feeling, isn't it?

Have you ever had that feeling where things are finally coming together? Where it finally clicks and you've conquered something you initially struggled with?

Years ago, after I discovered I wasn't going to be happy in a career in Accounting & Finance, I set out on an adventure to master the art and science of coaching. I had a big dream of running my own business, bringing color to people's lives through having powerful conversations.

A few years into my journey, I was still struggling and hadn't made as much progress in mastering coaching as I had expected. I spent most of my time lost and overwhelmed in coaching sessions, to the point I wasn't even sure whether it was for really for me. And I wasn't the only one. Some of my coach friends were struggling in the same way, and quite a few gave up and applied for jobs.

I stuck with it, and got to a point where I could consistently get extraordinary results for my clients. I remember those sessions where that ability was fresh and new. It was such a thrill! There's almost nothing better than getting a handle on something that used to be so confusing and frustrating.

If you're not there yet, and you'd like to consistently get extraordinary results in your coaching, then this book is for you.

In my experience, the path to mastering the art and science of coaching doesn't have to be dragged out. The process of getting to a level where you get solid results can definitely be sped up. Being frustrated by my own journey, and fed up with watching other coaches go through similar ones, I decided to figure out how coaches could get to expert level faster, which would increase their confidence and help them charge a healthy fee for their services. Here's what really got in the way of getting there faster:

1. Imagine this scenario: You ask your client the first question "What do you want to get out of this conversation?" and your client starts sharing their story. They might give you 2 or 3 examples and after a few sentences you start to wonder

whether you'll be able to remember everything that is being shared with you.

This split second wondering means you've missed some information, which only makes it worse. Then, you need to ask your next question...after you feed back what you've heard. But you don't remember. And what is your next question?

It's very easy to get lost and overwhelmed in a coaching conversation. As a coach you are not only dealing with your client's stories, you are also dealing with the stuff that goes on in the back of your mind. The internal dialogue that takes your presence away from what your client is saying. And on top of that, you are trying to follow the structure of a coaching session in the way you've learnt in your coach training.

2. Coach trainings run anywhere from 2 (really?!) to 14 (sometimes more) training days. One thing that over 90% of my clients complain about is the fact that they go to these trainings and have high expectations of success. The energy at the training is motivating and uplifting. Then they come home, back into their own environment and poof, "now what?".

Without a platform for ongoing support to continue integrating what you've learnt, your skill level quickly drops. Sure, you can practice with peers but with everyone at the same level you are still guessing whether you are practicing right, and as a result your progress is slower than it could be. And what happens when you then get stuck in a coaching conversation? Your confidence level takes a beating.

3. Most coaches are perfectionists and take on responsibility for their client's outcome. And this leads to procrastination.

"Am I good enough?" It's a question most coaches ask themselves. The funny thing is that the "good enough" is often the same as having to be "perfect". If you combine that with a huge sense of responsibility for their client's outcome, and procrastination is your new best friend. Now, procrastinating out of fear is not a fun place to be. What makes it worse for a lot of coaches is that they feel they have to be successful in their lives, and otherwise they feel like a fraud. Or they are afraid others will think they are frauds.

What happens as a result? You don't go out and practice coaching. You don't charge (much) for your services. And you don't ask for feedback (even though you know that feedback is the food for champions) in fear of not being good enough.

I'm here to help you change that. One of the major differences for me (and my clients) in mastering the art and science of coaching, has been the Quantum Leap Coaching Template that I hold in mind while coaching. I really didn't set out to create a system or a template for myself, it evolved over years of figuring out the structure of change. Participants at coach trainings always asked me how I could remember everything my client said and not get lost. That's how I discovered I was using a system. In this book I will take you through all of the phases in the system and how to use it to consistently get extraordinary results for your clients.

PS. This book comes with a free online toolkit. You can find it right here: https://www.thecoachmentor.org/ql-toolkit

Femke Mortimore

My name is Femke Mortimore. My mission with the The Coach Mentor is to provide a platform for coaches that is easily accessible, sustainable, and fun for those who are dedicated to unleashing the very best in their clients.

In this book I will teach you how to break down any overwhelm in coaching and to consistently get extraordinary results with your clients. I discovered my love for coaching shortly after I started as a management trainee with ORMIT, a management development organization in the Netherlands. My second assignment was at a meat packing plant where I was part of a team that worked on improving the efficiency in the organization. As part of my role, I had to train and coach the team leaders of the different divisions. Even though I had no clue how to coach (honestly, they were more pleasant conversations than anything else), I truly loved the idea of bringing out the best in someone through conversation.

With a master's degree in International Business, I obviously lacked the skills for coaching. I started with the NLP (Neuro-Linguistic Programming) practitioner and master practitioner in 2002. Driven by my strong sense of purpose, I spent much of my free time in trainings. After I received my certifications I assisted on about 7 or 8 practitioners and master practitioners, and then went to NLPU to get my NLP trainer's license.

Yet, I still felt that something was missing. I was now able to run patterns on people, and what to do with clients in certain situations. What I didn't know, was how to structure an entire coaching program. How did transformation actually work? And what would make it last? In my search for answers, I found the Meta-Coach training system. In 2005 I went through that training and gained an understanding of change and transformation that I didn't have before. Why, then, did I still feel a lack of confidence?

This was true for others who had gone through the training, and many of my NLP and Meta-Coach friends/colleagues eventually gave up on their dream to coach. That just didn't seem right.

So I started a journey to figure out how to make it simpler, yet more effective. After years of developing my skills and helping coaches work on honing theirs, the Quantum Leap System organically grew out of my desire to streamline the coaching process and how I trained coaches.

As you might have guessed by now, I am passionately dedicated to mastery in the field of coaching. From the very beginning I have felt a strong sense of responsibility to those I coach. If I am going to help my clients unleash their best, I want to be my very best both in my attitude as well as in my skills. What I love even more than coaching itself, is teaching others the art and science of coaching. I aim to give my very best to my students so that they can give their very best to their clients.

If you have any questions about the book or its contents, please feel free to write me at Femke@thecoachmentor.org.

{ Part 1 }

Introduction To Coaching

Definition of Coaching

"If an egg is broken by an outside source, life ends. If an egg is broken from the inside, life begins." – *Jim Kwik*

In 2015, James Robertson, then 56, made the news. Why? Because the Detroit resident, while taking the bus part of the way, walked about 21 miles round trip to work every day. His '88 Honda Accord had broken down 10 years prior and James makes this trek 5 days a week in all kinds of weather.

You might wonder why I am sharing this story with you. After all, we are talking about coaching here. Well, this is a powerful metaphor that explains what a coach really is.

Nowadays, anyone can call themselves a coach. There are lots of different kinds of coaches; Health coaches, soccer coaches, voice coaches, leadership coaches. Not all of them help their clients in the same way. And that makes it really confusing. Not only for people who could use the services, but also for coaches themselves. *How are you going to know what skills to apply and where the boundaries of your field of your profession are if you don't have an understanding of what coaching is and what it is not?*

There are a lot of different interpretations of the word, so let me explain where it came from. In the 15th century, the wheelwrights (a person who makes or repairs wooden wheels) started building horse drawn vehicles with a steel-spring suspension. These carriages were more comfortable and people were able to get to where they wanted or needed to be far faster. These "carts of Kocz" started to spread through Europe quickly and eventually gave rise to the term "coach". A coach being a mode of transportation that takes you from point A to point B. *The fact that you don't have to walk means that you will get there a lot faster, with less effort or struggle.* And that's what coaching does.

Image 1 - Coaching as a mode of transportation

The term first appeared in the academic field in 1830, when Oxford used it as a descriptor of a tutor who "carried" a student. In the 1860s it started to be used in sports in England. It wasn't until the 1970s, when Timothy Gallwey wrote his book The Inner Game of Tennis, that the term made its transition to interpersonal coaching.

There has been a need to define what coaching does in the interpersonal field. Dr. L. Michael Hall defines it as follows: "Coaching is the art of facilitating the processes within an individual or organization to a specific, agreed upon outcome, by means of a ruthlessly compassionate conversation that gets to the heart of things — the client's core meanings — and thereby identifying and mobilizing inner and outer resources for generative change that leads to develop, unleash, and actualize the client's potentials for achieving his or her dreams.

Whew. That's a mouthful, is not it? Let's break this down into bite-size pieces.

First of all, coaching is the art of facilitating. What does that mean? It comes from the word facile, Latin for "easy". What we do with coaching is the art of making change easy.

Ultimately this is not getting your client from a physical point A to a physical point B, but they are in a specific state; A specific situation where they want to be able to behave differently, think differently, act differently so that they get a different outcome.

As coaches we make that process of getting to where our client wants to be, easier. We are the '88 Honda Accord that James Robertson had before it broke down. We do this through understanding the structure of their current experience, and comparing that to how they would like it to be, so they have access to different behaviors. This means that we are not interested so much in the content of our client's story, but rather in *how* they have created their reality.

The second part of the definition relates to "an agreed upon outcome". What you work on is not based on what you think your client needs to get out of the session. Rather, it is based on what your client decides he wants and needs to get out of this session. This starts with asking "What do you want to get out of this conversation?", and continues with gathering high quality information to get to the heart of the matter.

You help your client gain enough awareness so that they know where the change power is, and can make an informed decision as to what to work on in the coaching session.

We do this through having a ruthlessly compassionate conversation. Coaching is more than just having a kind gently loving conversation. While that's is definitely part of it, we want it to be "ruthlessly compassionate", meaning that we are going to be challenging our clients to move outside of their comfort zone from a place of compassion.

It is more than likely that your clients have operated from within their comfort zone. And even though it is not necessarily very comfortable, making the change might be scarier than leaving where they are at right now. As such, we need to create enough safety (through compassion, love, care, etc.) to then be able to challenge them to move outside of their comfort zone, based on their own desired outcome.

The next part is "fleshing out the core meanings of the client and identifying inner and outer resources". What goes on in the back of someone's mind? What beliefs hold them in this specific place? What inner or outer resources are needed to make a shift and what new core meanings do they need to go from where they are to where they want to be?

How do you flush out those core meanings? How do you identify inner and outer resources? And how do you then help your client implement them so that they can actualize their potentials to achieving their dreams. That's essentially what coaching is; You are making easy the achievement of your clients' dreams based on an agreed upon outcome. In order to identify that, you need to understand and master what makes the process easy. That's where **The Quantum Leap Coach System** comes in. I will share more about that in the next part of this book.

What coaching is and is not

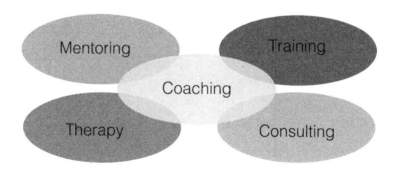

Image 2 Different helping professions

Coaching is a helping profession. It is not the only helping profession out there. Understanding the different types of helping professions will give a clearer distinction as to where the boundaries of coaching are.

Consulting

Coaching is not consulting. When someone hires us as a consultant they expect that we have a specific expertise and based on that expertise we are going to be *giving advice*. That's the skill of this profession. Something we mostly steer clear of in coaching, because we believe that the best and most transformational answers come from the client. That does not mean that we never give advice. On the contrary. At times it can be very helpful to do so in a conversation. When we do, we make it tentative and to the outcome.

Mentoring

A mentor has experience in a specific field and they *guide* their mentee. Essentially they take someone by the hand and show them how to do something they have mastered.

Training

In training we transfer knowledge. What we are doing is the skill of *teaching* and that's different from coaching because coaching we don't want to teach.

Therapy

Now the last one is counselling. It's not uncommon for people to confuse coaching with counselling. From a coaching perspective we see the client as already whole. They have enough ego strength to face reality the way it is and are therefore able to be challenged and confronted. They are not broken.

In counselling a person still needs to heal from something that happened in their past. Assume that they get to a level of nothing taken away from them and that's the place where coaching comes in because coaching ultimately about moving from good to great. That does not mean that in coaching there is no pain from the past. Something might be holding your client back from achieving their hopes and dreams, but they are able to face it and deal with it.

Overlap

As you can see in the diagram, the other helping professions overlap a little bit with coaching. While the majority of your role as a coach is about facilitating process through asking questions, giving feedback on what you see/hear/feel, etc., there are times that you need to add in training, consulting, or mentoring. When, for example, your client is using a certain language pattern that distorts their reality, you can teach your client about cognitive distortions. It provides a frame for your client to understand what they are doing. It helps with creating the awareness they need to make a decision on what needs to change. Without that little bit of teaching, the process can take a lot longer.

If, however, your client needs to learn a skill or gain understanding about a specific area of expertise that you don't have, then you refer them on to a trainer or mentor. Being able to make the distinction between coaching and the other helping professions, allows you to keep your skill and your profession clean. This, in turn, ensures that your client has the right expectations of what it is that you do and what it is that you don't do.

In addition to the helping professions mentioned above, there might also be medical or neurological issues that affect your client's mind-body-emotional state. In a TED talk Dr. Daniel Amen explains what he learnt from 83,000 brain scans and how the brain affects your mood. He gives examples of NFL players (American Footbal) with poor brain function who have been put on a Brain Smart Program and how 80% of those players improved their mood, memory and blood flow. He also talks about a 9-year old boy with extremely violent thoughts (drawing pictures of himself shooting other kids), discovering a cyst on his brain the size of a golf ball. While these are extreme examples, they illustrate the fact that our brain has an affect on how we feel and behave, and that medical issues shouldn't be ruled out as avenues to explore when your client comes with topics like depression, suicidal thoughts, etc.

Process Facilitation

As explained earlier, facilitation means "to make easy". Our focus is on process. The process of change. That means we are not listening for content, we direct our attention to the structure of how language is used, the beliefs that hold emotions and states in place and that keeps your client from doing what they want to do.

The Quantum Leap Coach System helps you stay focused on the process. In addition, there are a few guidelines that support this.

Image 3 Guidelines that help make coaching easier

Make sure your client is coachable

Is this person coachable? Is your prospect able to self-reflect, open to feedback, and willing to look at reality the way that it is? If not, your client might need some training or counseling first, in which case you can refer them to a trainer or therapist.

Make sure it is something that your client can't do for themselves

Why would your client pay you money if what you are going to help them with is something they can do for themselves? The answer to that may sound obvious, but it's easy to forget to check with them what parts of the change they can already do. Your coaching will be most powerful when you make this distinction.

Make sure it's in your client's control

There is a difference between a desired outcome, and a desired effect. The latter can be something that involves others, like making a sale or getting a great outcome in a team project. We can only help our client change something that is inside of their control, which then maximizes the chances of achieving the desired effect.

Find what has the greatest change power

Since coaching is systemic, the journey of change can be made easier by finding where the leverage points are. You get leverage when you change the parts of the system that will ensure the other elements fall into place as well. When you don't get to the core of what needs to shift, it can take your client a lot longer to get to where they want to be and the chances of regression are far greater.

Make sure there is enough "energy in the system"

Energy comes from the drive to want to change, the commitment, as well as the embodiment of the new experience. The more your client can feel their new way of being and behaving, the better off they are to make the change stick. In addition, when there is enough motivational energy in combination with the decision, this will solidify it even more.

Simplicity is key

Did you know that one of the most important principles of Taoism was named after Winnie the Pooh? If you did, you probably read "The Tao Of Pooh". I actually think it was the other way around, and that the cute little bear was named after P'u, also known as the Uncarved Block principle.

In Chinese, the word P'u means simple or natural. In Taoism, it is a symbol of simplicity. "And the nicest thing about that simplicity is its useful wisdom, the what-is-there-to-eat variety – wisdom you can get at." There's something to be said for useful wisdom. It's easy to over-complicate things with adding more knowledge and greater detail.

In a previous career, I was assigned with building a new cost pricing system both in concept as well as the implementation of it. A cost pricing system basically calculates the manufacturing cost of your products. This means that every cost an organization makes is allocated to the different products and services. A big part of this is labor cost, ie. the amount of man hours that are being spent on making the product. The question then becomes to how much detail you want your employees to track the time they spent on the different services.

To most that's boring stuff. I mean, it was bad enough to have to suffer through math classes during high school, right?! Well, it so happens that I love math, so this was a dream assignment for me. But stick with me, I'm getting to a point here soon. Gathering this information helps managers and directors make decisions on where to improve their processes. However, if you go into too much detail, you run the risk of micro-managing and making it too complex.

When I went to visit one of the financial controllers in the business units, he wanted me to structure the time-keeping system in such a way that his employees could keep track of every 5 minutes they spent on a particular product. He also wanted a long list of activities to keep track of.

Are you starting to feel overwhelmed when reading this? Good! That's exactly what I want you to feel. This is what it's like to overcomplicate things. If I had given him what he wanted, his employees would have gotten frustrated by the amount of time it would take them to keep track of their time. What's even worse, is that he wouldn't have gotten the necessary information to make informed decisions.

This is exactly why a lot of coaches get overwhelmed. They don't know what information (details) to filter for. And often they get introduced to many different models and lists as part of their coach training, which is more information to keep track of. All this does is slow down the learning. The idea behind the Quantum Leap system, is simplicity. To bring the structure of coaching to its natural state. And while that doesn't mean that it will not take time to learn the skill of coaching, it does mean that you can do it much faster.

Image 4 Simplicity is key

One way I did that, was by integrating all the coaching models I know into 1 model. I also applied the 80/20 principle to bring down the amount of knowledge you need to know in order to excel as a coach. In my experience, it has been more like 95/5 than 80/20.

State Management – The Somatics and Semantics of Coaching

"To learn to think independently of the barrage of environmental stimuli is a skill that, when properly executed, will change the brain, the mind, and the body to prepare us for the future.

If emotions brand experiences into long-term memory, then when we are faced with current obstacles in our life that require thinking and acting in new ways, and we use familiar feelings as a barometer for change, we will most certainly talk ourselves out of our ideal. Think about this. Our feelings reflect the past. But to change is to abandon past ways of thinking, acting and feeling so that we can move into the future with a new outcome. To change is to think (and act) greater than how we feel. Emotions like fear, worry, frustration, greed, and self-importance are familiar feelings that, even in the midst of transformation, if we decide to succumb to, will surely point us in the wrong direction."

– Dr. Joe Dispenza

In coaching there is an ever greater awareness of the importance of neuroscience. Neuroplasticity is a term that describes the process in which many structures of the brain can be modified by experiences. It's the ability rewire the brain and we keep this ability for our entire lives.

There are a couple of things worth noting here. The first is that memories are imperfect. They are not a perfect account of what happened, and our narrative can change over time. This is usually something that happens out of our awareness. In coaching it is something that we consciously do. By reshaping our memory of previous experiences, we reinvent our past and as a result, our present and future.

The second is that our emotions are strongly connected to how we form memories and the narrative we construct around a specific event.

Thirdly, imagining and doing are the same thing. Studies have shown that we can build up our muscles by mentally rehearsing that we are lifting weights. When we do so, the same neural pathways are activated as the real experience. This is why coaching has the most impact when we help our client get into state and help them see, hear and feel what they want to see, hear and feel in real life. It sets them up for generating change.

And the last point is that experiences transform the brain. New neural connections are made and this starts to inform our body in a different way. This is exactly what we want in coaching. As such, we are not only focusing on the cognitive aspect of change in coaching, but we need to use the entire mind-body system to affect the desired change.

Image 5 Coaching is about the entire mind-body-emotion system

Being able to do this well (using the entire mind and body), will set you apart as a coach. The more vivid and "alive" the experience is in our body, the greater effect it will have on rewiring our brain. The great news is that we can reformulate and repattern our neural connections to change how we feel, and open ourselves up for new behaviors. In Part V of this book I go over the core coaching skills. In it, I will explain in more depth how state induction brings together the mind and body to set your client up for success in the desired change.

Part I Focus Points

* *The skill of coaching is process facilitation. This is different from mentoring, consulting, and therapy, which focus on guiding, advice giving, and healing.*
* *Guidelines that support making change easy: focus on the process, make sure the client is coachable, that they can't do it for themselves, that it's within their power to make the change, find where the change power is first, and make sure there's enough energy in the system to make and solidify the change.*
* *To learn coaching and get to great skill level quickly, you need to focus on simplicity rather than trying to learn everything at once. Learn the 5% that will get you 95% of the results and focus on an easy-to-use system.*
* *Lasting change brings in not only the cognitive but also the somatics. Change needs to occur in the entire mind-body system. In coaching this is done through state management.*
*

You and Your Client

When I was about eight years old, we got a little Siamese kitten. When she was six months, my mom had told me and my brother to keep the door shut. Mei Ling was not to go outside. Of course, the absent-mindedness of two young kids in combination with a cat in heat spells trouble. So one day she got out.

The three of us (my mom, my brother and I) went out of the house to try and catch her before she found herself a "friend". Mei Ling hid under a car. I was told to approach her slowly, but in my eagerness to catch her I ran towards the car with my hands reached out.

She took off.

I had failed at winning her trust. A big whoopsie!

Building trust with your client is, in a way, similar. Of course, I don't expect you to run after your client with your hands reached out. That might be a little bit creepy! The way it often shows up in coaching, is when you interrupt while your client is still talking or when your energy is a lot higher or lower than your client's is.

Similarly, if you try to confront and challenge your client before helping them feel safe, you're not going to get very far.

At the heart of great coaching, is how you show up as the coach and how to relate to your client.

You, The Coach

Coaching is an intimate profession. We get up close and personal with our clients, and this affects not only our client. It touches us deeply as well. At least, it has the ability to do so. Since we are holding the space for those we help in their transformation, the way we show up determines our ability to facilitate greatness.

Emotional intelligence, compassion, empathy. These are obvious traits (skills) to hone as a coach. So is being able to release judgment and stay curious. In addition, we need to have a willingness to hold accountable, set boundaries and confront. So often we are comfortable with one or the other, and have a hard time doing both at the same time.

On the one hand, our client needs to feel safe enough to speak his truths. Speaking candidly about our feelings and thoughts, firstly to ourselves and then to another human being, is not always easy. Particularly when it comes to the "darker" side of our thoughts and emotions. It takes a level of safety to do so; A knowing that we are not going to be judged, that there is a sense of unconditional positive regard.

As coaches we are holding the space for our client to be this truthful, and this then puts us in a position to confront and challenge our client. We confront them on blind spots, incongruencies, and taboos. We also confront them on the paradoxes that often occur when we try to avoid something: that we are actually creating what we don't want. Confrontations can be painful, because it calls on us to admit to the things we feel uncomfortable with.

This dance between love and care on the one hand, and confrontation on the other, requires from us coaches that we show up fully present, in a know nothing state. At the foundation of all of this, from what I have witnessed over years of working with coaches, is unconditional self esteem.

Phrases like "I am not important", "I don't matter", "I am not good enough" are a common occurrence when I talk with coaches, and they have a negative effect on how we apply our skills. Mistakes become taboo. We discount the skills we have and hide our emotions. Consequently, we get distracted during our coaching sessions. Our attention goes inward to our own thoughts and feelings, not where they are supposed to be; with our client.

Image 6 Self doubt takes away from being present with your client

Self esteem, then, is the first topic we will focus on in this chapter. Once we have a solid sense of self esteem, we can then focus on releasing judgment and the know nothing state. In addition to having a solid sense of self, so that we can show up with curiosity and care, there are several other things we need to work on. Part of knowing nothing, means letting go of preferences we have for certain types of emotions and thought patterns.

Becoming aware of the emotions we favor or taboo, as well as styles of thinking, allows us to pick up more cues from our client. Instead of ignoring or deleting what we don't like, we are able to witness it and feed it back when appropriate. That's the power of truly being in a know nothing state.

Image 7 Coaching requires a know-nothing state

The Role Of Self Esteem In Coaching

There are a couple of conversations that I remember vividly from when I first started coaching. While I don't remember the topic my clients were discussing, I remember the sweaty palms, my staggered breath, and my mind racing a hundred miles per hour thinking how I could save myself. "Save yourself from what," you might ask. Well, mostly from myself.

One of the examples was when I was doing a demonstration of a coaching pattern. Jason struggled with his boss. He would draw a blank every time he felt he was put on the spot by his manager, and he wanted to be able to clearly state his opinion in those situations.

He and I sat in front of a group of about 10 people. As I asked questions, Jason drew a blank. He was doing his problem right in front of me, because he felt that with an audience and me asking questions he was put on the spot. I had no clue that was going on. I figured it had to do with the kinds of questions I was asking. I must be doing something wrong!

After about five questions and "I don't know" as an answer, I started to draw a blank myself. We simply sat there like two deer in the headlights of a semi-truck, unable to move, think, or find a way out. In the back of my mind I wondered what the participants would think about me: I don't know anything yet, they'll never take me seriously. They will think they wasted their money on me. How am I going to get out of this?

Eventually I had to accept that I did not have the skills to help my client transform this dragon state, and so I stopped the conversation. I owned my lack of ability, and explained how the process is supposed to work. Paradoxically, it was my honesty through which I gained respect from my participants. More importantly, something happened inside of me. I realized that my stuck-ness wasn't about me. It was about my abilities. Separating the two made a huge difference.

Let me make this distinction a little clearer for you: there are three self concepts that play a role in your role as a coach: self esteem, self confidence, and self efficacy. Self esteem is defined as the opinion one has about their value as a human being (person). This is different from self confidence, which is the belief that you have in yourself and your abilities. Self efficacy speaks to your belief about being able to do a specific task, and the learn what is necessary to be able to perform even if you don't know how yet. The most important distinction between self esteem and the other two self concepts, is that one speaks to the human being and the others are about human doing.

Too often we confuse them. We are what we do. We have confused who we are with what we do, feel, think, and say. When this is the case, making a mistake means that we are putting our sense of value on the line. Tim Goodenough, in his book *"The Gamechanger Protocol"*, describes 3 levels of self esteem: healthy, conditional, and low. He has identified that there are certain absolute beliefs that drive healthy (unconditional) esteeming of self, which are often the very opposite in those who have low self esteem.

An absolute belief is unconditional in nature, which means they are true regardless of the situation you are in. As such, those beliefs need to be healthy in every circumstance. Someone who has a healthy self esteem, has these 10 absolute beliefs in place at the CEO level of the mind (meaning they are at the highest possible level):

I am ok.

I take full responsibility for what is mine and let go of what is not.

I matter.

I belong.

I am enough.

I have what it takes.

I fully accept all of myself.

I am good enough.

I am a work in progress.

I am worthy of connection, love and belonging.

When we take an unconditional sense of self value into a coaching conversation, it is ok to make mistakes. We don't have to worry about what our client will think of us. It won't affect our self worth.

Of course, our self confidence may not be at the level that we'd like it to be as beginning coaches. Our skills are still developing, so it wouldn't be realistic to be confident about them. Being comfortable with conscious incompetence creates the freedom to practice, learn from our mistakes, and as a result, accelerate our mastery of the skill.

The Know Nothing State

In coaching, we don't want to impose our own perceptions, beliefs and values on our client. Our map of the world does not come into play, unless perhaps once we are already in the phase of creating the change where we can give menu lists of options for our client to try on. Other than that, our mapping needs to stay out of it. Any self talk in the back of our mind, expectations, jumping to conclusions takes away from asking great process level questions.

Being in a state of know-nothingness means the attention is on the client, and his/her strategies, focusing on understanding their model of the world without having an opinion or expectations about it one way or another. Our ability to access this state is dependent on self esteem, as well as releasing of judgment, embracing emotions, stretching our meta-program preferences, and clearing any cognitive distortions.

Releasing Judgment

We need judgment in our life. In fact, it's imperative to our existence to judge situations, others, our opinions, etc. However, in coaching it stands in the way of merely observing and asking the necessary questions to uncover how they've mapped out their experiences.

Because of the fact that our experiences are psycho-logical, not merely logical, more often than not we are unable to predict what beliefs are driving our client's states and behavior. So jumping to conclusions – which is a form of judging – can be detrimental to the outcome of the conversation. It stops us from asking more questions and allowing our self and our client to get surprised by the answers.

When we judge our client for their thoughts or their behaviors or ourselves for our performance, our mind is taken away from what it needs to be focused on.

Embracing Emotions

Emotions are a chemical flush through your body that creates a mixture of sensations, and they are always right. Why? Because they are the result of the meanings that you've given to something, someone, a situation or event. When we look at emotions as information – they inform us how to respond. Our emotions can be over-reacting to certain stimuli, because we infused it with toxic and distorted meaning.

Certain emotions aren't comfortable to us, because we have given meaning to the sensations we experience in our body as negative. And so we need to suppress, ignore, or deny them. And that's when the emotion stops being informative. As coaches, we work with our client's emotions. As such, we need to be able to embrace them. If we don't, we aren't able to pick it up in our client, miss the fact that they are suppressing the emotion, or move away from it as fast as possible when our client expresses the emotion.

The more access we have to all emotions and sensations in our body, the better we will be as a coach.

Stretching Meta-Programs

As coaches, we will have preferences for certain styles of thinking. Our eyes and ears might be tuning into the big picture and disregard details, simply because we have an affinity for that way of thinking. Or we prefer to look for how things are the same, rather than for how things are different. In Neuro-Linguistic Program, these preferences in thinking styles are called Meta-Programs.

The problem here is that when we have a strong preference for one side of the spectrum, we delete the other side. When we are coaching, this means we can miss out on a lot of vital information that our client shares with us. Or it means that we don't pick up on the fact that our client is, in fact, stuck in the same thinking style.

Flexibility in thinking styles is important in the various roles we have as coaches (to detect patterns, to motivate, to confront, etc.) as well as in noticing when our client is stuck in a certain way of thinking.

Clearing Cognitive Distortions

Closely related to Meta-Programs, are our cognitive distortions. These play an important role in identifying what to change for our client, which will be discussed later on in the book.

What happens when you have distorted some of your meanings? Do you take it personally when your client is not getting results? Do you revert to blaming or labelling? All of this will take away from your ability to be present and truly listen to your client.

Building Relationship

Image 8 Building relationship

At the same time we build meaning around the concept of Self, we do the same with Others. Lucas Derks, a well known Dutch NLP pioneer, developed the Social Panorama model to explain how we build relationships with ourselves, others, and concepts in the mental space that exists around us.

Where we place others (near of far, in color or black-and-white, bigger or smaller than us, etc.) will determine how we stand in relation to them. Our feelings towards them are in direct relation to the position we have given them in our social panorama. Lucas states that the way an individual position him or herself in regards to others in their mental space "governs the better part of social behavior".

The relationship you have with your client will determine the outcome to a large extent. It's is a unique kind of relationship that it is intimate whilst at the same time we need to be able to be separate enough to not get lost in our client's emotions and story. We also need to be able to step back enough to focus on structure and patterns in our client's story.

How do we map this out in our mental space so that it can drive our relationship with our client in the best possible way?

Self Esteem

We already discussed this in the previous part, but your sense of self esteem is a key element of being able to show up as a coach who can hold the space and practice tough love when needed.

Love and Compassion

Unconditional positive regard, a concept developed by the humanistic psychologist Carl Rogers, is the basic acceptance and support of a person regardless of what the person says or does, especially in the context of client-centered therapy. This also applies to coaching.

Years ago, when I did a demo in front of a group of coaches, the lady who volunteered to be my client had to make a difficult decision. She was a single mom of a young daughter who very much wanted a sibling. Her best friend was gay and desperately wanted to be a dad. He had asked her if she wanted to help him make his dream come true.

The reason why it was so difficult for her was that she didn't want to. And yet, she loves these two people in her life so much that she wanted their dreams to come true. It had created an internal conflict for her, but after the coaching she realized she knew what she did and did not want. Her decision was made. When we had our break after the demo, a few participants came up to me and asked: "Wasn't that difficult for you, not to have an opinion about the topic?" No, it wasn't difficult for me. It's not up to me to have an opinion about my client's life or the choices they make. That's where unconditional positive regard comes in. Basically, you are applying the principle of separating human being from human doing, and looking through those eyes at someone else.

This is another area where releasing judgment comes in.

Ordinary Courage

Sometimes you need tell my clients something and they are not going to necessarily like you in that moment. It's a good thing that it is not your job to have them like you. You can't be focused on that, because otherwise you may not want to bring up things that are uncomfortable and painful. It takes courage to hold another person accountable, to speak our truth about what we observe.

Brené Brown mentions in *"The Gifts Of Imperfection"* that the root of the word *courage* is *cor*—the Latin word for *heart.* In one of its earliest forms, the word *courage* had a very different definition than it does today. She writes: "Courage originally meant 'To speak one's mind by telling all one's heart.' Over time, this definition has changed, and, today, courage is more synonymous with being heroic. We certainly need heroes, but I think we've lost touch with the idea that speaking honestly and openly about who we are, about what we are feeling, and about our experiences (good and bad) is the definition of courage. Heroics is often about putting our life on the line. *Ordinary courage is about putting our* vulnerability *on the line. In today's world, that's pretty extraordinary.*"

Responsibility To/For

Even though a coach helps their client get an outcome, they are not responsible for it. It's easy for the lines to blur. As a result, you might be working harder than your client.

Making the distinction between response-able to and response-able for means that you can hold your client accountable and identify what they need to work on in order to help them reach their outcome.

Colin Cox and Lena Gray, two master NLP trainers in New Zealand, explain this concept by saying that everything that goes on behind my nose and toes, is mine. Everything that goes on behind your noes and toes, is yours. It's about owning your powers of thinking, feeling, speaking and behaving and realizing that your client also has these powers.

Part II Focus Points

* In coaching you need to both create a safe space for your client to speak their truth, and to confront and challenge to help them move out of their comfort zone.
* Permission to coach comes from building relationship, and that starts with your own state management as a coach.
* Our own state is dependent on our level of self esteem. Great coaching is also founded on the releasing of judgment, the ability to let go of your own map of the world, which is done through stretching meta-programs, clearing cognitive distortions, and embracing emotions.
* Relationship is built through the lens of unconditional positive regard for self and others, having the courage to give feedback, and having clearly established boundaries of responsibility to / for.

{ Part III }

The Quantum Leap System

It is easy to get overwhelmed with all the story your client shares with you. They are going to share with you their thoughts and feelings in relation to something that is incredibly important to them. Something they probably have not shared with anyone before. Thoughts they weren't consciously aware of before working with you.

Often, they'll want to share the full story, give you all of the details, in an effort to feel heard. They give you one example after another. It might also be that your client does not know where to start. There are so many aspects to the outcome, that they jump from one topic to the next. In other words, it's a chaos in their minds and it comes out that way as well. It is up to you to make sense of it. To organize the information your client shares in such a way that clarity emerges.

Just think of of it as putting together a puzzle that has a 10,000+ pieces. You open the box, turn it around and all of the pieces spread out over the table. Where are you going to start? If you don't have a system for organizing putting the picture together, you are going to be completely overwhelmed and lost.

Worse yet, if you have the puzzle, but not the template of what to work towards. It'll take you forever to finish.

It's very similar in coaching. You are going to get an overwhelming amount of information and if you don't know what information to highlight and ask questions about, how certain pieces relate to one another, etc., you'll be hard pressed to help your client gain the awareness they need to make an informed decision on what they want to change, let alone actually making the change.

You need a system. A way to structure the information so you can use it effectively.

The Quantum Leap is a visualization of all the elements that play a role in transformation. It allows you to keep track of what information you have, what's missing, and where to go next. **It starts with organizing your client's information**. The ability to organize comes in handy in coaching. Your client shares most of the information with you through language. And it is not structured in a way that easily helps you figure out what the two of you need to work on.

It is up to you to put it in a structure. And that inevitably raises questions like: What information do I filter out? How do I remember all of it? How do I structure the information? How do I choose what to ask questions about? Without organizing the information, you will get overwhelmed and start chasing your client's words.

Putting the information in a structure allows you to:
- know what information you have
- start seeing connections
- know what information you don't have, so you know what questions to ask
- keep track of the conversation (and have a better memory of it)
- utilize the information in the change process

There are three important elements in structuring information:
1. Categorization
2. Visualization
3. Story-telling (Building connections)

Categorization

Categorization is the process of placing something into a class or a group. In NLP, we call this "chunking up." We ask the question "What is this a part of?" or "What is this an example of?"

Of course, in order to answer these questions, you need to have an idea of the different classifications there are. The Quantum Leap system gives you an overview of the different groups and classes that information can fit into, and explains the relationship between all of them. Since all elements are related, the act of grouping your information will help you see the big picture. It also helps you to chunk down from the big picture, and sideways.

An example of the latter would be when your client starts talking about a different outcome. That would be a sideways jump, and when you can identify this you won't have to chase your client to the other outcome. You can simply make them aware that you hear a different outcome (allowing them to either confirm or not) and help them make a decision as to what to work on.

Three meta-programs are at play here: Global(General)/Detail, Options/Procedure, and Matching/Mismatching. Using the Quantum Leap system requires synergy. The ability to look at details through a larger picture (meta-detailing) and the ability to stay flexible while you procedurize your options. In addition, in order to be able to categorize, you need to sort for sameness as well as for difference. You need to, for example, be able to recognize that your client is talking about two different present states. They are the same in that they are both present states, yet different in the sense that they occur at a different time, in a different context, and with a different response. As part of the larger picture, they might be related to the same overall outcome (meta-detailing). Together, these work to keep you focused on the outcome instead of getting distracted by your client jumping from one topic to another.

This helps you in deciding what information is most important to work on (which you can confirm with your client), since you are unable to process all information right away. Mapping it out and classifying the information means that you can store it easier, and get back to it at a later time. Your client can, therefore, jump from present to desired state with you following their energy, without it getting you off track. Unless, of course, it is on an entirely different topic. At which point you can point that out and get back on track.

Visualization

Visualization and categorization go hand-in-hand. In order to keep track of all of the information you are organizing, it helps to put it in a visual template. Neuro-Scientist John Medina says: "Hear a piece of information and three days later, you'll remember 10% of it. Add a picture and you'll remember 65%."

The beauty here is that you don't have to make up the picture in your own mind. Your client already has done this for you! All you need to do, is ask the right questions so that you can start seeing what your client is seeing. As you build an image of what your client is seeing, hearing and feeling, you can jump in and out.

Making connections / Building the story

"Most people try to remember information with their sense of sound. They will repeat the information over and over again, hoping it will somehow stick. Sound is very limited because it does not attach easily to other memories. A sound is also always sequential; If you want to remember something with sound you have to start at the beginning and work your way through the information. However, when you see information as an image in your mind you can jump in and out of the information, and therefore improve your understanding, too." – Unlimited Memory, Kevin Horsley

In the process of classification and visualization of your client's story, you can start making connections. How is what they say connected to the story that you have been building so far? And how does it relate to the structure of change? (To be more specific, how does what they are sharing with you, relate to their level of motivation, decision, figuring out the "how" of the change, etc.)

Kevin Horsley, who is a world-record holder when it comes to memory, shares that "when you see information as an image in your mind you can jump in and out of the information." *This is exactly what we want to do.* When it comes to the present and desired state of our client, we go 2nd position with them. Knowing all of the elements that need to be present in order to fully go 2nd position, we can gather more information by realizing what is missing. And it helps us to identify where the change power is, by asking testing questions.

Beyond going second position on our client's present and desired state, we also jump into the bigger picture of the Quantum Leap system. Do I now have enough motivation? Has a decision been made, and is it ecological? Do I have the "how" of getting from where I am to where I want to be? *If not, those are questions to be addressed.*

Here is a step-by-step overview of how to categorize, visualize and jump in and out of the process of change for your client.

1. Understanding and recognizing the different elements

In order to be able to classify information, you need to be able to identify what a certain piece of information is a part of.

2. Using the elements to step into the story

You can only do this if you have enough details. This is why "grounding" the conversation is important. If you don't know what your client is seeing, hearing, and feeling in their body, it is hard to step into their story. As mentioned before, you don't need (or want to) be make pictures in your own mind. In coaching we come from the premise that our client has all the answers and resources.

If you find yourself having to make up or fill in some of the blanks, you need to ask more questions. This is where the next step, testing the story, comes in.

3. Testing where you are in the story

With this step, you need to be able to tell the difference between filling in the gaps with your own information and using your client's information to build the story. Do you know how to tell the difference?

As human beings we are very adept at filling in the gaps based on what we already know or understand. We use our own mapping. And this usually comes with a great subjective sense of certainty, on which we then act. Starting to notice when you "fill in the blanks" will help you in becoming better adept at asking the questions necessary to build your client's story and not your own.

This is also where confusion becomes your ally here. If you are confused, it is a matter of figuring out what information is missing, so you can ask the right questions. Filling in the blanks might make you feel better (more certain) in the short run, but it leads to confusion later on. That's a different kind of confusion, one that is based on misunderstanding rather than an awareness that you don't have all the relevant details yet.

Overview Of The Quantum Leap Template

In part II of this book, I talk about the importance of being in a know nothing state. Another way of saying that, is to start with a blank slate. Rather than having any preconceptions about where your client needs to go or what they want, assume that you know nothing. The way I visualize that, is by imagining a blank canvas in my mind, to my right and a little bit higher than my head. That's where I start any coaching conversation, and from there I will "build the story". This is at the core of the Quantum Leap system.

Image 9 Every coaching session starts with a blank canvas

As you'll have read in the introduction to coaching, in every coaching session there is a present state and a desired state. This is at the very foundation of Neuro-Linguistic Programming. In 1987 Robert Dilts, one of the early developers of NLP, and Todd Epstein noticed they were intuitively using a more effective method than their advanced NLP students for mapping out problems and designing interventions to get to solutions. As they explored their own process, they found that the way they were viewing the structure for problem solving included 5 components: Symptoms, Causes, Outcomes, Resources, and Effects. This is how the SCORE model was born.

It begins with a present state (with symptoms and causes), a desired state (with outcomes and effects) and the resources (the how) needed to bridge the gap between the two. The Quantum Leap follows this structure, and adds in some additional pieces for you to be able to get to where the change power is for your client.

First, we want to understand how our client has created their problem and what their outcome would be like. That means you need to get their strategy (story) for both. Without that information it's hard to move on to the other elements in the system.

Image 10 Getting to know present and desired state

Looking more closely at the strategy, each of these states are in relation to a specific trigger within a specific context. E.g. you might be really comfortable in sales conversations (context), except for when your potential client asks you for the price of your services (trigger). Your client will then respond to this trigger with thoughts and feelings, and builds a matrix of meanings around it (L. Michael Hall) that ultimately drives their state and which, in turn, drives their behavior. Gathering this information is what I call "building the story". From this information, you'll be able to replicate their internal experience in a given situation.

As you are listening to your client, you can start identifying these different elements of their story. Are they talking about the present or desired state? Are they introducing a new present state or is it related to the one you are talking about? Is this a belief that holds everything in place? Is this a symptom or a cause? (This is why the skill of categorizing and organizing is so valuable.)

Putting all of this information in the template allows you to start seeing the story of how it is now, and of how your client would like it to be. This, in turn, will give you the opportunity to feed it back to your client, which ultimately leads to the awareness they need to identify the leverage point, build enough motivation to want to change, get to choice point, etc.

Without awareness, your clients won't be able to make an informed decision about what to work on in the coaching conversation. Awareness comes first from building the story of how they are creating their present state.

This is phase I of a coaching conversation: Building the story.

The strategies for both PS an DS of what your client wants to be coached on are just the start of the template. An important start, but there's more. The next aspect, is identifying the gap. This is where you run through a process of detection and analysis (Phase II). This helps you pinpoint the leverage points for change: What specifically needs to change so that your client achieves their goals? Your ability to detect patterns, limiting beliefs, and anything that stops your client from getting their outcome, takes the coaching session to a whole new level.

Image 11 Detection and analysis

Once you've done detection and analysis on the gap, you can make a list of steps to work on (Phase III – The How). Out of this list, there might be steps that your client can do for themselves or where another helping profession (such as training or mentoring) is needed. In helping your client distinguish between steps that they need coaching on and those they don't, you'll get really clear on the work the two of you have to do together.

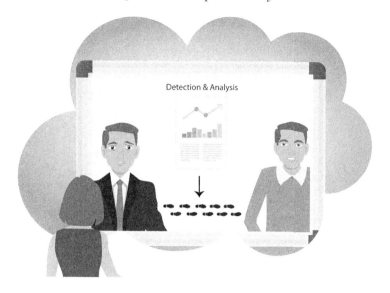

Image 12 Figuring out how to create the change

Having grabbed a hold of the leverage points — so your client is informed on what to change — there are several "energies" that need to be activated to drive and solidify the transformation. These are motivation and decision (Phase IV – Setting The Outcome). Without it you can start to work on creating the change, but you might find that your client does not do the actual work that is necessary to implement it. Inevitably with a big dream, when it starts to become real and things get hard, motivation is what moves us through. Supported by a strong commitment.

The process of decision making goes hand in hand with making sure that the change is ecological. When you change your beliefs, your behaviors, it will not only affect you. It will also affect your relationships, your finances, and other areas of your life. If an outcome is at the expense of other areas in your life, or perhaps of other goals, then this needs to be weighed into the decision of whether or not to move forward with the change. This process might also lead to a more well-formed outcome by incorporating any objections that might arise from asking the question "Is this outcome ecological in all areas of your life?"

Image 13 Getting a decision on the outcome

When your client has made a decision, you can set the outcome statement along with several KPI's (key performance indicators) that lets you know when you've achieved the outcome. Once you've locked this in, you can start with the actual change work (Phase V – Getting The Outcome). Part of this is testing your outcome once you've done the change work. This phase is where it all comes together.

Image 14 Bringing it all together to create and solidify change

In summary, these are the phases of the Quantum Leap template: Strategy Process (present and desired state); Detection and Analysis ; Figuring Out The How; Setting The Outcome; Getting The Outcome.

Let's take a closer look at the different phases.

Phase I – Building The Story

In this phase we are looking for the strategy process of where your client is and where he/she wants to be. As we gather information from our clients, we can start to make connections and build the story they've created for themselves, and help them write another one.

There are some distinct pieces of information we need. These are the elements of the strategy process: Context; Trigger; VAK / Semantic Space; Beliefs (Meta-States); State ; Behavior.

Image 15 Building the story (strategy process)

In image 15 you can see what that looks like. In the context of cold calling (the red phone), when the client looks at a list of people to call on his computer (trigger) his mind goes to a reference experience of being bullied (VAK) and has the following beliefs: I'm not good enough, they'll laugh at me, they'll know I am a failure and it'll always be that way (beliefs). This puts the client into a state of fear and as a result he watches tv instead (behavior).

Context and trigger

Where, when, and with whom does your client want to effectuate a change?

This information keeps you focused. It'll be something to come back to when you find your client strays off topic. Without this information, you might be able to get the desired state and you can even induce your client into that state. However, will they then be able to access or maintain that state when confronted with a specific trigger in a specific situation?

Asking for an example will help you stay focused and ground the conversation in a context so you can find the trigger and take it from there. It's common for a client to want to share several different examples. Since coaching is about structure and not about content, you don't actually need all that information. In fact, it takes precious time away from getting the strategy process.

You can explain this to your client by saying something like: "What would be a powerful example of this? We will use that to uncover the structure so that we can find out what needs to change. We can then test that in other situations as well. For now, let's stick with one example."

Beliefs

To uncover the beliefs that hold a state in place, you can ask meta-questions. These are questions that inquire about the thoughts and feelings your client has in relation to an external event or thoughts and feelings inside of themselves. It's the higher level beliefs that drive our state which, in turn, drives our behavior. Ultimately, what we want to know is how our client is (or needs to be) thinking and feeling about the trigger that puts them into a specific state.

You can read more about these types of questions under the Skills section of this book. Here are a few examples of questions you can ask:

* What do you believe about x (the trigger) that makes you feel insecure?
* What conclusions have you drawn (about yourself, the situation, the other person involved)
* What reference experience comes to mind?

In addition to asking questions to uncover the beliefs, your client might be offering them up as they share their stories with you. The question then is: Do you hear a belief when your client shares it?

We know that beliefs don't have to be true to be believed, and at times your client can make so much sense that it can be hard to distinguish a fact from a belief simply because they are not seeing that difference. So when they share something, it's said as a factual statement rather than a belief. It is up to you to make that distinction. This is easier to do when you are in a "know-nothing" state.

State and VAK

The result of the way we think and feel, is our state. It 's the sum of our physiology, our thinking, and our emotions. By inquiring about the state our client is in, or wants to be in, we start grounding the conversation. Naming the state also helps your client to step back from it. Adding the specifics of what they see and hear while in that experience, it allows your client to step back from it even further.

Your client will, for the most part, be unaware of how they've created their problem. They may have some idea of what is going on, and they might even have thought of a solution. Most of the time, this "fix" comes from their problem thinking. The reason for this is that they believe their beliefs to such an extent that they don't question them. It's operate as their truth. What you'll often find as a result, is that when your client starts answering questions they get hypnotized into their problem state.

Any answers you will then get are from within their problem state. This is something to pay attention to, because you won't be getting any valuable answers from this place. When you notice that this is happening (often because you are going around in circles), you can ask your client what state they are in right now. Are they doing their problem right now? What this does, is help them take a step back so they can start to reflect on that state.

Ideally you want your client to step in and out of their problem state so you can unravel the structure of how it works for them. The same applies to the desired state, though here you might need to help your client get into the state. This is also when your ability to think out of the box and help your client dream up a state that they couldn't have imaged from inside of their current way of thinking and feeling.

Semantic space

The representations we build of the world around us, is not two-dimensional. It's not just flat images. We use the mental space around us to map out our visual, auditory and kinesthetic representations. In other words, our relationship with concepts like time, others, self, etc., is built not just within us but around us. You'll notice this when your client is talking about the past and they keep pointing in the same direction every time. Or about a specific person and they keep pointing to an imaginary person as they talk about them. This is called "semantic space", the space where we create meaning.

It's an important part of getting the strategy process, which is why we listen with not only our ears, but also our eyes and our bodies. When we use second position to step into our client's map of the world, we will be able to understand how our client has created their state. This often helps us get an idea of whether we have the important pieces of the story. This is discussed in more depth under the Skills section of this book.

Behavior

Our behavior (our actions and our words, including tonality and speed of voice) is the external response to a trigger. Usually there is a desired behavior that our client does not have access to in relation to a specific trigger. This is the result of how we respond internally, unless of course we need to obtain a certain skill.

In coaching, our main focus in on the first option. And as such we use the behavior as part of the test to see whether we have reached the outcome.

Let's see what this looks like, using an example. Below there are two stories. They're Jessica's stories. The first one is where she is right now. The second one where she would like to be.

Story #1

Jessica is building her coaching business. She is fairly new as a coach, but knows that she can make a difference in other people's lives. The other day she had a sales conversation. She felt so insecure and uncomfortable that she stammered and had a hard time formulating her sentences. There was a whole lot of uhm-ing going on.

Reflecting back on it, she realizes that she started off feeling confident. She'd say it was even at a level 8. And she kept it that way until closer to the end. It was when her prospective client asked her about her price.

She had set her price beforehand, but she feared what the other person would think about it: "She's going to think it's too much." This led to a series of other thoughts, like "What if I can't deliver? She'll see that I am a fraud. I am not good enough to charge money. I am not good enough. I am a failure."

When we had identified her beliefs, a memory appeared of when she was seven years old. She had been playing a game of jump rope and was the only one out of her friends to not be able to jump in. She drew the conclusion that she was a failure right there and then.

Her confidence made way for insecurity and as a result she lowered her price, and stammered while she shared it. She didn't make the sale, and she'd had quite a few experiences where this had happened. She wondered if she was ever going to be able to build her business.

Story #2

Jessica is in a sales conversation. She's been asking great questions and identified how she can help the prospect. After explaining how she can do that, she gets the question: "How much does it cost."

The question reminds her of a couple of different coaching conversations where she made a difference for her clients. In the back of her mind she thinks: "I still have things to learn, but I know I can already make a difference. And the price I have set reflects the value I have to offer. This person needs to decide whether it is worth it. I know I am good enough."

Maintaining the confidence she had throughout the entire conversation, she states her price in a matter of fact way. Then, she leaves a silence so the prospect can think about it.

Below, you can see an illustration of the two stories. On the left hand side is story #1, the Present State. And on the right hand side is story #2, the Desired State.

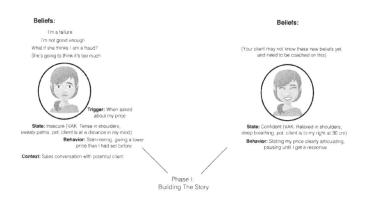

Image 16 Phase I - Building The Story

In both of the above stories the situation that Jessica finds herself in, are the same. And yet, the outcome is different. This all depends on how he responds internally to the situation. For now, something triggers Jessica to play out the first story. And what she really wants, is for the second story to be a reality to her.

When we are coaching a client, we start with building these two stories with our client. First, we need to know the context and the trigger that the story is set in. *A trigger is either an internal or external event that kicks off a series of internal responses (images, beliefs, meanings, etc.) which result in a state.*

From this state we respond with our behaviors (words and actions). This can either be effective or it can be ineffective, even harmful. Knowing that the trigger is not the problem, we need to change our response to the trigger in order to have access to a different set of behaviors. Taking a systemic approach, both the present and desired state are held in place by all its different elements. In Phase I our goal is to understand how the system works. What happens between trigger and the resulting behavioral response?

It's important to note that your client will offer up a lot of this information, just not in a structured way. It's up to you to build a structure out of this by picking up on the different pieces and putting them in a process. If your client goes to beliefs first, you can follow them there and start mining for the layers of beliefs. After that you will be able to gently guide your client to get the other elements of the story. The beauty is that you don't need to follow a specific set of steps. You can simply follow the information and then ask questions to gather the missing pieces.

Phase I Focus Point

* Always choose ONE specific context /example for present (or desired) state, even though the client wants to give us many examples. Your client may think they will feel heard after sharing more and more stories, but this is not what helps them get results.
* The trigger will be the same from present to desired state. Your client might want to change the trigger, but this doesn't stop it from occurring in their life.
* Put a label on the state – name it. This helps you to identify the different present or desired states, if there are more (which there usually are).
* Ask meta-questions to find the beliefs for the specific context
* Try on the beliefs so it makes sense to you. If you don't have enough information and find that you have to make things up, you need to ask more meta-model, clarification and meta-questions.
* Confusion is great – it teaches you to get more information by asking more questions
* If looping around in circles – there is usually more than one present state or that the conversation in not grounded enough
* This is NOT a linear concept – you will skip from one phase to the next and back, or on to another, throughout

the conversation. It depends on where your client's energy is. It's a dance between following your client where they are, and leading them to where they wouldn't naturally go.

* Learn how to organize information – you already to this in many aspects (like knowing where to put the knives, forks etc)

Phase II - Detection and Analysis

Going back to the core of coaching, which is to facilitate (make easy) lasting change, then the question is: "What change will make the most impact".

What is it that we need to work on? So often when your client states their desired outcome for the session, it is not what they really need to be working on. That's why we start with building the story and create awareness of what is going on and where to go instead.

Your first question for every coaching session is: "What do you want to get out of this session (or coaching program)?" 95% of the time, the answer you get from this question, is not the outcome that you need to be working on. Instead, we want to get the what behind the what. We want to get to where the change power is: that one element that if we change that, it is going to make the rest of the change easy and the client is going to step into performance and action a lot easier.

What I mean by that is that your client can come in and say "Oh, I want to work on a plan." and as you gather more information you discover hat he already has a plan. He is just not executing it, because of perfectionism and fear of failure. You want to be working on the latter two, because if you just take the plan as the outcome, you won't be making much of a difference for your client. He will still procrastinate and not take any action. Getting the "leveraged" what means that you are working on the outcome that is "hidden" behind the initial outcome or solutions your client sets. When we start coaching too soon, because we have identified something to work on with our client early on in the conversation or we just go with the first thing our client brings up, then we run the risk of not having identified the very thing that is capable of changing the system.

Tim Goodenough, in his book "The Game Changer Protocol", describes this concept powerfully: "Not all beliefs are created equal. Beliefs are held at various levels of power in your mind. Imagine being a New York skyscraper with every floor holding beliefs about all sorts of things. Beliefs held on different floors are often linked. The higher up you go, the more powerful the beliefs are. The beliefs that reside at the top of the skyscraper, where the CEO suite is normally situated, have power over the beliefs at lower levels. This mimics how a CEO and his/ her executive team influence the entire company. When a CEO level belief changes, all the beliefs that are linked to that CEO level belief change too."

As we build the story of our clients "hero's journey" (present to desired state), we can start to identify the higher level beliefs (regardless of whether that's mapped out in images, sounds, words, etc.). This allows us to step back, and go through a process of detection and analysis with our client so that we can find where the change power is. To get to this leveraged "what", we need to detect and analyze how the stories differ. What does it take for us to be able to detect patterns and identify beliefs? There's two parts to this.

First, how easy is it for you to spot the difference in the following images?

Image 17 Spot the difference (image by izakowski)

One aspect of detection and analysis, is the ability to spot the differences between the present and desired state. You are using the same skills and thinking styles as you use for analyzing the image above. In addition to contrast analysis, there's the detection of limiting patterns: **"If x happens, then I can expect to see y as a result."**

If you've ever taken an I.Q. test, you'll probably recognize the type of question below.

If "New York" can be encrypted as PGYAQTM, how can you code the word CHARLOTTE?
EICSNPVVG
EJCTNQVVG
EICTNPVVF
EJCSMPVVG

Your ability to recognize patterns in coaching closely resembles the skill needed to answer the question above. Here we need to be able to both match for sameness and mismatch for difference. To be able to detect these patterns, **we need to know what we are looking and listening for.**

This is where for coaches the most time will be invested: informing ourselves of the different patterns can operate in our client, so that we can identify it when it comes up. What kinds of patterns can show up? What are all the elements that we can change in the system?

As you go through the process of exploring the present state and desired state (Phase I – Building The Story), there is actually a limited list of things you need to detect. The leverage point can be found in the different elements of the system (i.e. how the experience is created).

Image 18; Detection and analysis clockwise: limiting belief; limiting use of semantic space; problematic reference experience; troubling relationship with concepts; troubling relationship with emotions; cognitive distortions; limiting meta-program

Limiting frame (belief)

Oscar Wilde wrote: "A thing is not necessarily true because a man dies for it." Oftentimes we are so "married" to our beliefs that forget that they aren't necessarily true. In fact, very often we are not even aware of them! And yet, they inform us how to feel about something, someone, an experience, which in turn instructs us how to respond.

When we look at the structure of a belief, it is a confirmed thought. A thought can be entertained without it affecting our neurology in a big way, but when we give it credence by saying yes to it, that becomes a different story. We say yes to a thought in different ways. We can say yes with meta-stating it with an-other thought, about which we can then have another confirming thought. This solidifies it into a belief. Your client's present state is held in place by certain beliefs. By uncovering them through the use of meta-questions you can – together with your client – identify whether a belief is working against the outcome.

Troubling relationship with a specific emotion

Emotions provide information on how to respond to a given situation. Anger can be a necessary, powerful response to a violation of our boundaries. Feeling sadness allows us to let go of something we lost. Vulnerability allows us to truly connect with ourselves and others.

Your client may not have permission to feel certain emotions. Whether that's happiness, joy, sadness or anger, if your client disallows the emotion the energy will turn against him/herself. Teasing out the tabooed emotion takes careful listening with both your ears as well as your eyes. Is there something your client is avoiding? What can be seen but is not being said? Asking "Do you have permission to feel X emotion?" is the most direct way to find out whether this needs to be a topic of the conversation.

Troubling relationship with a concept

As with emotions, we build relationships with ideas. Simply hearing a word can trigger an intense state. If your client wants to be in a relationship, but the word commitment puts him/her in a state of fear then (s)he'll be having a hard time in reaching the desired effect. When you hear or see that your client has a strong response to saying a specific word (either through repetition, emphasis both in voice or gesture), this might be an indication that (s)he has a troubling relationship with that concept. That's when you want to explore that further and ascertain whether this is true or not for your client.

Cognitive distortion

Aaron T. Beck first proposed the theory behind cognitive distortions when researching how to treat clinical depression back in the 1950s and 1960s. It was David Burns who made it more widespread through the use of names and examples for the different distortions.

In short, our thinking can be distorted, which results in very toxic states. The problem with distorted cognition is that it "feels" right. And as such we can get very much lost in it. In listening to what our clients say, we want to train ourselves to picking up cognitive distortions. In Part VI of this book you can find an overview of the cognitive distortions.

To make it easier on yourself, you can provide your client with a list of the most common of distortions, so you can do the analysis of what to work on in the coaching session, together.

Meta-program preference

Meta-programs (aka thinking styles) tell you something about *how* a person processes information. In interacting with the world, we seek to understand it. For example, some of us can edit a letter or essay and miss lots of details whereas someone else will pick up every single error, however small it may be.

This has to do with the way we filter information. In this case, you can either be detailed oriented and mis-match information or you can be global oriented and match information.

Essentially, a meta-program tells you which information to focus on and which information to delete. Someone who is detail oriented does not see the big picture and those who have a preference for the big picture ignore the details.

Preference is the key word here. As we habituate a specific filter, we end up preferring it over what would be the "opposite" of that thinking style. We might even start identifying with it to such extend that we are unwilling or "unable" to do the other way of thinking.

And that's when we get stuck. When that happens, your clients will often think the solution is to do more of what they prefer. That's where you need to bring awareness to the meta-program through providing feedback and challenging them. They might not have permission to go to the other side, and that becomes what needs to be worked on. Or they may simply not have had enough experience. That's when getting a small reference experience where they did apply the desired thinking style can be useful.

An example of a small referent could be that when your client wants to do more internal referencing, and they strongly rely on the opinions of others for decision making, you can use a simple example like: "Who decides how much salt goes on your food?"

Even with a small example like this, your client can discover that they do have the skill for internal referencing. It's just a case of then mapping that skill over to the context in which they

want to achieve a result. How to do that, will be part of Phase III
– The How.

Use of toxic reference experience

During on of my first trainings I taught, one of the participants had a troubling relationship with the idea of cold calling.
He would freeze up at the very thought of it. When I asked him
a few questions about his present state, it turned out that he
used a reference experience of when he was 3 years old and his
parents were getting a divorce. There wasn't a lot of time for
playing and so he felt rejected. When thinking of picking up a
phone and calling someone, his mind kept going back to that
experience and that would set off limiting beliefs.

In situations where the reference experience plays a domi-
nant role, this can be the very topic to work on as a leverage
point.

Limiting use of semantic space

Imagine your client talking about something that they want.
You notice that every time they talk about the future, they point
to the right and behind them. At the same time, whenever they
talk about something that happened in the past, they point to
that very same direction.

This is an indication that they have given past and future the
same place. It wouldn't be hard to imagine then, why they'd say:
"I feel really stuck and just don't seem to be able to move forward." Meaning making is not just through words. We also cre-

ate meaning through using our mental space around us to map out concepts and build relationships with events, time, people, etc.

Years ago I coached a client who stuttered. He had placed fluent people as a group to the left from him. When I asked him to join that group, he was unable to even imagine it. While this wasn't where the change power was, it was an important part of his strategy process. In paying attention to where someone points or what consistent gestures they make when talking about something, you can start to uncover the way they have used their semantic space.

Too much meaning placed on a deficiency need

Coaching aims to facilitate the self actualization of people. Maslow described self actualization as a being need, at the top of the needs hierarchy. Once you've gone through the deficiency needs of survival, safety, social love and belonging, and self esteem by filling the deficiency, you move to self actualization. This last need is different from the other ones in that there is not a sense of "enough". Instead, there's a sense of continued yearning to contribute more, to be more, to express more of oneself.

Deficiency needs, once satisfied, drop away in the background. Until there is a deficiency again. If we get hungry enough, sleepy enough, cold enough, deficiency kicks in and that need gets our attention.

However, we can distort these needs. As such, food can become synonym for safety, for being loved, for having control, etc. It is not just about survival at that point, but we've infused it with important meanings. And as we do, the deficiency need starts acting as a being need instead. There's never enough of it and we keep wanting more of it. There's a preoccupation with it that stops us from being our very best, from focusing on the true being needs.

Lack of skill

It might also be that your client does not have the skills or the knowledge to do what they want to do in the desired state, in which case training is needed. As you go through your analysis, you might find that another helping profession is necessary for your client to achieve their outcome. In addition, it might be that your client does have the skill in another area but hasn't realized this on their own. Asking "Have you done this before? Perhaps in a different area of your life?" can be very powerful.

A while ago I was coaching a lady who wanted to learn how to prioritize and map out what to do first in her work life. She felt confused and overwhelmed. When I asked her that very question, she said that she does prioritize and know what to do first when it comes to puzzles. She loves doing puzzles with a large amount of pieces (around 10.000 pieces) First, she'd find the corners, then the four sides. And after that she would put colors together. That's how we found out she didn't need to learn how to prioritize, there was something else at play here.

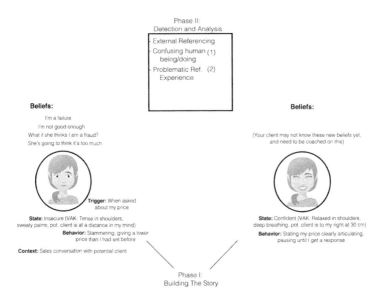

Image 19 Adding Phase II Detection and Analysis

An example of detection and analysis

Let's go back Jessica's stories in Phase I (see page 33). Knowing the stories, and having all of the elements, what is the difference between the two? What patterns can we detect? There are several points we can identify.

* External referencing (Meta-Program)

By making statements like "She is going to think it's too much. What if she thinks I am a fraud?" Jessica places high importance on what the other person will think of her.

* Confusing who she is with what she does (Cognitive distortion)

Her higher beliefs are "I am not good enough" and "I am a failure". Rather than it being something that she can or cannot do, she over-identifies herself with it, confusing who she is with what she does.

     * Problematic reference experience

Using a reference experience of not being able to jump in when playing jump rope when she was seven years old, and she couldn't, she creates the feeling of failure. It's not a useful referent.

    This process is a collaboration between you and your client. By feeding back the stories, you help them create awareness of how the system works. It often helps to give your client a list of cognitive distortions and meta-programs, so they can start to see if for themselves or recognize it when you mention what you've observed.

Phase II Focus Points

    * What elements in the system do we need to change? There are 7:
       1. reference experience
       2. limiting belief
       3. cognitive distortions
       4. meta-programs
       5. troubling emotions
       6. troubling concepts
       7. limiting use of semantic space
    * There are usually several things coming in way. You start to prioritize with testing questions. What is the

most important things to work on NOW – where is the leverage point aka the **change power**?

* By prioritizing you start building your coaching program because you end up with a list of what to work on in order to reach the desired outcome.

Phase III - The How

Having gone through Detection and Analysis, we are then ready to figure out HOW to get from now to a new now. Identifying the list of limiting beliefs, cognitive distortions, reference experience, etc., is the start of figuring out what to change. This leads us to identify the leverage points for change. We do this through a process of prioritizing which patterns and elements of the system will make the biggest difference.

Finding The Leverage Point

If we change one aspect in the system, the other parts will inevitable change as well. The question is whether the change we make will create leverage. Once you have a list of differences or patterns, you can figure out which of those would make the biggest difference and prioritize what to work on. Going back to the example I used in Detection and Analysis, this process of prioritizing goes something like this:

"Jessica, if you knew that you are not what you do, and felt that with your entire body, would that help you feel confident and excited as your potential customer asks you about your price?" If the answer is yes, you can then check to see how it would affect the other aspects, like the prophesying. This also gives you an opportunity to build on the desired state and make it more robust and complete, because you've identified something that your client had a blind spot for (the fact that she was confusing human being with human doing).

In the case of Jessica, the separation of human being versus human doing was where the change power was, and it naturally changed the limiting beliefs and need for external referencing. That's not always the case. It could be that it changes the limiting beliefs a little bit, but not completely. Even with the separation of who she is from what she does, the reference experience still felt like it was in the way. So that was another step to work on. This means that you can have several topics to work on with your client, out of which you can create a coaching program.

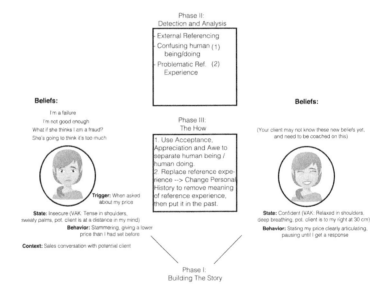

Image 20 Adding Phase III - Figuring Out The How

Once you have all of this information, you can dive deeper into the how of changing that particular element or pattern. It's only in knowing and understanding how the present and desired state differ, and what is the driving element in the system, that your client can answer the question "What do you need to do to get your outcome?"

This question is often asked too early, if it gets asked at all. When this happens, your client is not informed enough to give a high quality answer. More than likely, you will get answers that are performance based rather than focused on what needs to change in the inner game.

While in Phase II – Detection and Analysis you focus on identifying where the problem could be, in Phase III you look for what could be the solution. At the same time that there is a shortlist of what you might detect in your client's story, there is also a shortlist of what you might need to do with your client.

Image 21 Figuring Out The How (clockwise): Install new beliefs; clear cognitive distortions; stretch meta-programs; add in resources (meta-states); change use of semantic space; change reference experience; delete limiting belief

Find and install new beliefs

With a limiting belief, you can help your client brainstorm new, more enhancing beliefs to use when relating to a certain trigger. You might already have some preferred processes you use to install new beliefs. If not, you can find some great patterns for this in Part VI of this book.

Reframe or refuse old beliefs

At times, before we can install a new belief, we need to get rid of some of the old ones.

Change reference experience

When your client uses a reference experience that's not useful, changing it to include a new one can be where the change power is. Sometimes this includes giving new meanings to the situation, and exploring other reference experiences that would serve your client better. Often this works together with changing the location where your client has put the reference experience and clearing cognitive distortions.

Change use of semantic space

One of my clients experienced high levels of stress because she had so much to do and she couldn't organize or prioritize all of the tasks. It was just too overwhelming. What we uncovered, was that her timeline was so short, that she could not see the individual tasks. When we extended her timeline, her whole demeanor changed and she was able to start planning things out. Change can be as simple as changing the use of semantic space. To solidify this, brining in new meanings about the change will help.

Meta-state with resources

Bringing in new resources, such as acceptance, appreciation, calmth, love, humor, and looking through the eyes of these states at the situation and our responses, can bring about a transformation.

Stretch meta-programs

When there is a strong preference for a certain thinking style and you've found that this is where the change power is, you can help your client by stretching the meta-program so they have access to that way of thinking.

Clear cognitive distortions

Clearing up cognitive distortions allows your client to give more realistic and empowering meanings to a triggering event.

In Part VI of the book, you will find a list of patterns and processes that you can run with your client, depending on what you have detected needs to change.

Let me give you another of prioritizing and figuring out the "how" of the change.

Jack is coached by Chris. His outcome is to be more confident when he is coaching executives. When Chris asks him what he means with more confidence, he says that he wants to be focused and without fear. Here we have information about the present state: fear. It turns out that this fear comes up before the coaching session, not during, and Jack has set a few rules for himself; He has the expectation that he has to be able to deliver on what the client is paying him for, and his mind goes to a fear of getting stuck (what if the client says "I don't know", and then I don't know how to deal with that) and ultimately this would mean he is a failure. We are starting to get a picture of how Jack is creating the fear, though we still need more information about what he sees, says to himself, etc., to be able to really understand how he is creating his fear.

The desired state is confident and focused. And as he is talking about what he wants, he says: "I need to allow myself to make mistakes, because all great coaches make mistakes." There is a powerful clue in this sentence, because he apparently does not currently have permission to make mistakes.

When we take a look at the information that we have here, there are 2 things that stand out. He is confusing what is does with who he is (I am a failure if I get stuck in a coaching session), and he does not have permission to make mistakes. He also made a complex equivalent where making mistakes equals failure, and he is prophesying (projecting a bad outcome in the future).

All of this is detecting and analyzing what is going on. Once we have all of the elements that are at play, we want to take a look at what would make the difference. Chris inquired about Jack's permission level to make mistakes, which was at a level 2.

So here we can start testing. **If it was at a level 7-8, would that allow you to be confident and focused before and during your coaching sessions? What would happen to your fear.**

If working on permission level solves the problem, great! If not, it might make a difference but there are other parts that need to be worked on as well. So then, we look at some of the other elements. If failure was just something you did, not who you are, would that make a difference? Or having a different relationship to the idea of failure? **Ultimately, we want to figure out what is going to make the biggest difference.**

Working through this can also bring up new limitations or blocks that haven't come up yet in the conversation. In that case you can add that to your list. Let's say that permission is what gets in the way. Now we are ready to figure out HOW our client is going to feel that permission.

This is a process of finding out whether your client already has a successful strategy for this, even if it is in another area of their life. When your client does not have a strategy for it, you can use your library of NLP and Neuro-Semantics patterns and suggest a solution. But this is only when your client does not know the solution for themselves.

These two questions help you test whether your client already had a strategy in place:

Do you know how to do this? / Can you do this?
Have you done this before?

The "can you do this?" and "have you done this before?" questions lead to more specific information about the client's resources to bridge the gap. If they can do it for themselves, then what do they need you for? Since coaching is about helping your client with something they are unable to do for themselves, we need to make that distinction.

If they know how to do this, but only in other contexts and not in this context, then it's a case of mapping over that skill. The key to doing this might be in finding new beliefs, so your client has access to the skill. It could also be that you need to change out a reference experience or stretch meta-programs. You will need to figure out what gets in the way of your client using that skill in the desired context.

Mapping Out A Coaching Program

It is during this phase of figuring out HOW, that you can start to map out a coaching program. Of course, here we are talking about only 1 present and desired state where you can identify several aspects to change. When you are setting up a coaching program with your client, there are usually several different contexts in which a change needs to occur in order to reach the outcome. In that case you use the entire process of the Quantum Leap template for additional states as well. Your client does not necessarily stick to the one present state. They might jump from one to the next, as they discuss their goals with you. To manage this, you can have several sheets of paper, and when your client goes to a different present state (that is part of their overall outcome), you can write that on a separate page. The beauty of it is that you don't have to chase your client from one story to the next. You can park a specific topic and let your client know you'll get back to it later. This means that you can stay on track whilst your client still feels heard.

Phase III Focus Points

* **The How** is where you ask most of your testing questions. You can also do a little bit of training (ex separating human being from human being) – would that make a difference? Can you do this? Have you done this? Is this in your power?
* Some of the steps / list of things will be things we don`t coach on as they already know how to do it (ex: I need to make plans, setting frames and already know how to do it)

Phase IV – Setting The Outcome

There needs to be enough energy in the system to create and solidify change. In their book "*Meta-Coaching Volume I*", Michelle Duval and Dr. L. Michael Hall propose that the two energies to prepare your client for change, are motivation and decision.

These two energies are interdependent and mutually influencing, where motivation addresses the big enough why and why not for making the change. The decision making process goes deeper into the (potential) consequences of changing or keeping things the same. The weighting of these consequences will be influenced by the level of motivation.

Michelle Duval and Dr. L Michael Hall have placed motivation on the towards/away from meta-program. What this means is that the energy of motivation is activated when there is a big enough why not (away from) of the present state, as well as a big enough why to move *towards* the desired state.

Paradoxically, even though your client can experience stress and discomfort from their present state, it's often also their comfort zone. It's what is familiar. And leaving it means increased risk, something our brain is naturally wired to avoid.

Studies have shown that most people are twice as sensitive to potential losses than to potential gains. This leads us to being more risk-averse. At the same time human beings are great at making the uncomfortable comfortable. Or at the very least bearable. Situations that are initially unacceptable eventually become the new normal.

This combination of avoiding risk and numbing ourselves to the uncomfortable reality, is what keeps us in jobs and relationships far longer than we should. It stops us from making the change we are really after. The dream we really want.

We are deluding ourselves that sticking with the status quo – however miserable – is the smartest and safest course of action. By talking up the risk of taking action, and discounting or denying the very real price of playing it safe, we give up the possibility of creating a future that is infinitely more rewarding. This process happens outside of awareness. We are unconsciously making decisions this way.

This places importance on helping your client find the internal motivation to change, and base their decision making on a well-informed weighing of the possible pros and cons. It is important to note that the decision making process might bring up new topics to address in the coaching, as your client might be distorting the potential consequences (think worst case scenario thinking). So as we go through this, we will also go through detection and analysis of the decision making process.

Motivation ⟶ Decision ⟶ Agreement

Image 22 Setting the outcome

Motivation

Achieving a goal, especially a "big hairy audacious" one, requires the ability to persist through obstacles, and endurance to keep going despite any difficulties that may arise. Just having the desire, is not enough. What we need, is motivation.

This is defined as the process that initiates, guides, and maintains goal-oriented behaviors. It's what causes us to act.

"The term motivation refers to factors that activate, direct, and sustain goal-directed behavior... Motives are the "whys" of behavior - the needs or wants that drive behavior and explain what we do. We don't actually observe a motive; rather, we infer that one exists based on the behavior we observe." -- Nevid, 2013

If motives are the "whys" of behavior, we can combine a big enough why with a big enough why not to create a propulsion system that keeps us going even when the going gets tough.

Finding A Big Enough Why

The main question you'll ask here, is "why is this important to you?" The answer to this question could be either stated in the positive or negative, and that's ok. If it's negative, you can ask your client: "So if you don't have this, what would you have instead?" Alternatively, you can just continue to go up the layers of importance by asking the same question (Why is this important to you?) about the answer they gave.

Example:

Julia wants to start her own lactation consulting business. She needs to leave her current job at the hospital, where she is not happy.

Coach: Starting your own lactation consulting business is important, because?

Client: Then I can decide my own time schedule.

Coach: And what is important to you about being able to decide your own time schedule?

Client: That gives me more time to spend raising my kids.

Coach: Imagine being able to spend more time on raising your kids. What is important to you about that?

Client: I'll be the mother I want to be.

As you can see, the higher up the levels we go, the more important the intention becomes. This is also where you'll see your client get more and more into state, because the higher up the levels of belief you go, the deeper it is felt in the body. This is how we create enough "Why" energy for your client to have the pull to go towards their outcome.

In case your client has a hard time answering the question, here are a few alternative ways of asking the same question:

What will that give you?

What difference will that make for you?

What will that open up for you?

What does that allow you to fall in love with?

Finding A Big Enough Why Not.

By helping your client take a step back from their present state and then quality control how they keep themselves in it, you build a strong enough "why not". It drives the desire to move away from where they are right now.

These are the kinds of questions you can ask:

* If you continue to do this for another five years, what will this cost you?
* What has it already cost you? And what is the cost of that?
* Does this make your life a party?

Like with the big enough "why", you build up the layers here as well. That way you'll get the most motivational energy activated in your client.

Decision and Ecology

When there is enough motivation to make the change, a commitment still needs to be made. The decision will effect other areas of your client's life and this needs to be taken into account up front in order to make sure that the change is ecological. Your client needs to make an informed decision based on tentative predictive thinking of the possible consequences of the change, both positive and negative.

If your client is expecting the worst to happen, even though this is highly unrealistic, then they'll make a decision based on their distorted thinking. One of my clients was afraid that if she'd go for being herself, she'd lose all of her family and friends. It was getting in the way of truly committing to an outcome that was really important to her. It turned out that she was using the reference experience of her mother yelling and shouting at her and she made the decision a long time ago to blend in and, in her words, be colorless. Once we had worked through this, she was able to fully commit to the change.

On the other hand, your client can also be overly optimistic about possible consequences. Imagine them wanting to leave marriage and they are convinced that their partner has also fallen out of love. They want you to help them prepare for telling their spouse and they are convinced that their partner will be accepting of it. Yet, the response they get is one of shock, pain, and refusal to accept the news.

At this point your client is not prepared for the emotions and responses of their partner, and they are overwhelmed by a feeling of guilt and confusion. Being overly optimistic means that your client is not looking at all the potential effects, and is therefore incapable of making an informed decision.

Part of making a decision, is knowing exactly what to make a decision on. What is it that you are going to change? After that, you want to weigh the pros and cons, so you can make a final commitment to either go after the change or not. Motivation plays a role in this as well, because it'll have an effect on the weighting.

Working through this, particularly before starting the transformational journey with your client, will prepare your client to deal with some of the consequences of the change. It also puts them in a position of ownership for taking action, to which they can then be held accountable.

Ultimately, what you want from your client is that they are able to wholeheartedly say "yes" to the change. Once there is enough information on what to change, and the potential consequences of that change, you'll be able to ask for that commitment:

* Will you do this?
* Are you going to do whatever it takes?
* Are you sure?

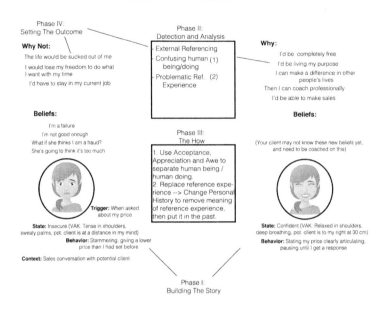

Image 23 Adding Phase IV - Setting The Outcome

Key Performance Indicators

Part of setting the outcome, is setting up the ability to test to what extent the outcome has been met. We call this a Key Performance Indicator, which is a quantifiable measure to evaluable the success of an objective.

When you've gone through the Quantum Leap template, you'll already have this information.

The formula for the key performance indicator is: Trigger (set in a specific context) + Internal Reaction + Resulting Behavior = Outcome.

If your client is able to respond, both internally and externally, to the trigger in the desired way they have achieved their outcome. This is information that you are gathering in phase I and refine it more and more as you go through the other phases.

Examples:

* When my husband raises his voice to a level 8 (trigger) I will be able to feel calm (slow breathing, relaxed shoulders, listen to what he is saying, ask myself "What do I think of this?" and make a decision about my opinion. I will then state my opinion speaking
* The first thought when I wake up in the morning after the alarm goes off (trigger), is "I wonder what will

happen today that I can be grateful for?" and feel excited to start my day. I get up and do my yoga exercises.

* When a prospect asks "How much does your product cost?", I look at my pricing structure in my mind (placed on the right hand side a little higher than my head), compare it to the needs to my potential client, make a decision which option is best and state my price with confidence (voice at level 6-7, short sentences).
* By the end of this coaching session, I am able to envision standing in front of a large audience (100 people or more) and see people with neutral faces and their eyes on me.

Phase IV Focus Points

* Define the outcome statement – it's usually not the same as the client came with in the beginning.
* Need to define the energy to do the change. Find the WHY / to and the WHY NOT / away from. The pros and cons and the consequence.
* It's not always the questions that gives you the information – you need to listen for the information given and then ask questions to generate more energy

* Often we're comfortably uncomfortable. Good at keeping the status quo. We need the energy to WANT to take a decision to make a change.

* A lot of times it's good if the coach really plays out the why not "I think you should just stay here, it's so easy for you" so that the client is really saying NO – I want to change (this is state induction)

* Are you 100% committed to do this change?

* If you are able to...... (feed back everything you have discovered about the trigger, internal responses and behavior) will you get your outcome? This will be the KPI

Phase V – Getting The Outcome

Once you have gone through all the other phases, this phase becomes a cinch. You've mapped out what to do in the Detection & Analysis and How phases, so you know exactly what to do. Whether it's saying no to old, toxic beliefs and replacing them with new ones, changing the location of a relationship, the concept of time, or using a new reference experience, this is where we are creating the change.

We do this through brainstorming, helping our client find answers through giving menu-lists, testing to see what is needed to make the change. This is also the phase where you put NLP and Neuro-Semantics patterns to use. When something needs to shift and your client (in the How phase) has been unable to identify how to get from A to B, you can use your experience of the different patterns to choose which one would fit with the change your client needs to make.

If, for example, your client has confused who he is with what he does, then you can take him through the Self Esteem pattern or work through the Game Changer Protocol. If your client has a problem with where they've positioned their partner in their social panorama, you can use one of the social panorama exercises that have been created by Lucas Derks. Part V of this book provides you with an overview of patterns that you could use in your coaching.

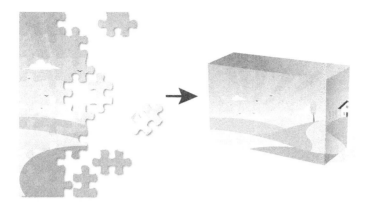

Image 24 Phase V - Getting The Outcome

Tasking

The faster your client gets to act on their new mental and emotional mapping, the better. This will help them solidify the change and integrate it in their neurology.

An important question to ask at the end of every coaching session: "What will you do to make this a reality of your life." Or, "What steps will you take to implement this." "What is the first thing you'll do to make this part of your life." Based on what you've worked on, your client can set their own tasks. You can also help them with some suggestions.

When you are testing the outcome, you then have something to refer to and hold your client accountable to. If they don't do their tasks two times in a row, then that needs to become a topic of the coaching conversation. Without taking action, there's no real change.

Testing The Outcome

The true test whether coaching has worked, will be when your client is able to think, feel, and behave in the desired way when in the situation where they previously had no access to these thoughts and actions. This is why you usually start with the testing process in the beginning of follow up coaching sessions. What worked? What didn't work?

As you go through this process of testing what worked and what didn't work, you might find new topics to work on with your client that previously hadn't come to the surface. At the same time, you can celebrate with your client the successes that have brought them closer to their outcome.

Ultimately, you want to get to the point where your client feels confident that they can get to the change. The meta-programs related to this process of testing, are matching/mismatching and counting/discounting. In addition, it is important to think in incremental steps, rather than all-or-nothing thinking. If your client focuses only on what is still missing, and discounts the steps that have been made, it's not going to feel like they are moving towards their outcome even when they are.

If your client thinks in all-or-nothing terms, it might be hard for them to count the progress they are making. It can go smoothly four out of five times, but when they "slip" and revert back to their old response, they think it hasn't worked at all. This is something to pay attention to, because it can sabotage the progress they are actually making. If you notice this as a pattern, it might be something to work on with your client.

Phase V Focus Points

* There are patterns to run on each of the **7** change elements, some are in the manual and there are so many more you can use / find.
* Having an arsenal of patterns and processes will make the process of change a lot smoother. It will initially help you with identifying the "How" phase, because it helps you understand the structure of different kinds of changes (for example how to install a new belief, build self esteem, set boundaries, etc)
* The sooner your client takes action on the change, the greater the chance of it being solidified. Letting your client set tasks with deadlines for themselves is a critical part of coaching.
* The tasks will also indicate how successful they are at the new way of thinking / emoting / acting. This is a great stepping stone for the next coaching session.
* Your own thinking styles play a role in whether you set tasks and test the outcome. The workbook that accompanies this book will help you identify which thinking

styles you need to stretch. It also has the process of how to stretch this.

{ Part IV }

The Quantum Leap At Work

Preparing For A Coaching Program

There is a big difference between coaching a coach and someone who has no background in this field at all. In coach trainings, we usually only get to practice with our peers. Unless that is your niche (as it is mine), you'll be working with someone who does not know the jargon that we're used to. They don't know what to expect, may not know how to answer your questions or what answers you are listening for.

This is a big part of the reason why have my mentoring clients work with coachees who don't have a coaching background, so they get a real life experience and I can pinpoint exactly what they need to work on to take their skills to the next level. How, then, can you ensure that you prepare your client in the best way possible for a coaching program. And what do you do the first couple of sessions so that you set yourself and your client up for success?

Preframing and Training

You will be asking questions of your clients that most of them have never been asked. Self reflection is not a skill many out there are familiar with. Nor is the fact that we own our own meanings and that we create our own reality.

The other day I listened in on a coaching session where the client had not been prepared in advance on what coaching is and what its premises are. She was playing the victim game, and had given her power away to where she felt very little influence over her life.

During a short interruption to talk with the coach, we had identified a strong external reference in combination with impossibility thinking. She was also using the past as a predictor for the future. The coach could now feed this back to the client. It didn't land. She was so stuck in her reality that she was unable to step back from it and see the patterns she was operating from.

While it can take a while before they see their own thought processes and behaviors, had it been explained to her beforehand that she creates her own meanings and that these meanings can be distorted, therefore creating a toxic reality, the coach would have made it a lot easier on herself as well as on her client. The tricky part is that if you don't prepare your client, you might break rapport when you start to go through the process of Detection and Analysis. This can lead to defensiveness..

I have prepared a PDF for you that outlines everything that your client needs to know before they get started with you. You can download it right here: https://www.thecoachmentor.org/ql-toolkit

You can edit it to fit your own style or feel free to pass the PDF on to your clients the way that it is.

Storylining and Getting The Lay Of The Land

During the first mentoring program I did where I sat in on a real life coaching session, the coach tried to follow the Quantum Leap system. After all, that's what we had been practicing all this time. Something was off, though, and she wasn't getting to where she wanted / needed to be. While she was getting some good information from the client, she was unable to get to the core.

This was a huge learning experience for me, because there is something different to those first one or two sessions you'll do with your client. *I call it story-lining and getting the lay of the land.*

When I first start out, I am not in a rush to get a clear answer on "What do you want." Nor am I very focused on getting all the details of the different present and desired states that we need to work on. Instead, I am starting to build the big picture of where my client is. This is what allows me to get to the core faster and it makes the rest of the sessions far, far easier.

Story lining is putting my client's stories on a timeline. What happened first, how are different stories related? So while I might dive deeper into a present state, a lot of the time that present state is a mere symptom and result of something that happened earlier.

To give you an example, the lady who was coaching during that first mentoring program, felt lost and stuck in her life. She was constantly worrying about her financial situation and did not know what she wanted in terms of a job. Her goal was to be financially free and have a job that brought in enough money to pay the bills and then some. And she wanted to enjoy her job. This is where the conversation started. Seems pretty straight forward. If you are solution oriented, you might think that we just need to help her figure out what she wants in terms of a job. Perhaps find her values, and then find a job that fits with that.

However, in doing some story lining, we discovered that the reason for her being stuck is that she has a problematic relationship with finances. She mentioned that she stayed in a troubled marriage for 13 years because she was worried about the finances. As a result of staying in the marriage, and allowing herself to be emotionally abused, she lost all her confidence. This, then, led to her giving her power away in other areas than just her marriage. Now we are starting to get a clearer picture of what is going on. And so is the coachee. This means that she will be far more capable of determining what she needs to work on and what outcome she wants to get out of the coaching.

First, we had to work on her relationship with the concept of finances. Second, she needed to get to know herself again. It's hard to say yes and no to something when you don't know your values. And then we needed to work on her level of confidence, so that she could increase the level of influence she felt she had over her life.

While we do think in terms of present and desired state in those first few conversations, usually it stays a little more at the surface. Paradoxically, it helps you get to the core faster, because while we didn't go into all the details of what she was hearing and seeing, saying to herself, etc, we focused on where the story started. That's where the problematic meanings are present. If they weren't, she wouldn't have been in the situation that she found herself.

First, you get the lay of the land and story line where your client came from, is right now, and where they want to be. Doing the Detection and Analysis on that, you get an idea of which present and desired states need to be addressed so that your client can get the best possible outcome.

When you give yourself the time to do this well in the beginning, you will get better results and save yourself a lot of time in later sessions.

Examples Of QL Coaching Sessions

Susan's Story

Unhappy in a 25-year relationship and struggling to find a sense of purpose after retiring, Susan wanted to feel more alive. She had the idea of starting a bed & breakfast, but she had no energy or will to get things started. *Initially, the description of what she wanted was vague. This is quite common, especially when there is a strong away from motivation in your client and when their preferred thinking style is global rather than detailed.*

Susan's outcomes played in the realm of relationship and work life. And her relationship seemed to be affecting other areas of her life to the extent that she felt stuck and lackluster. With a large outcome (feeling more alive), I usually start with a question like: "In what areas do you want to feel more alive" or "What does feeling more alive look like?"

She answered that she wants to get up in the morning and feel energized and motivated to do the things that she wants to do. She wants to go swimming or do yoga when she wakes up, and then start her day with the tasks at hand. Specifically, those tasks are working on her website for the bed and breakfast so she can get it online as well as decorating the rooms and getting those ready for guests. Through her answering my question, we have identified two contexts in which she wants to feel different in order to behave different. First, she mentioned the moment that she wakes up in the morning. And second, the tasks at hand. When asking her for a specific task, she chose the working on website texts.

There might be more. In this conversation I chose to explore these two in greater depth. I could have also asked her about other situations, but either way is can work.

Waking up in the morning.

Her current state when she wakes up in the morning, was passiveness. She described it as a state of paralysis, and a suffocating feeling as if someone is sitting on top of her chest. She's aware that there's sadness behind of all this. Her thoughts in that situation would go to: Nothing sparkles. There's no connection (with her partner). → This is not the way in which I want this. Nothing is really shared. It doesn't give me energy. Is this all there is to life?

Are you noticing how much information is missing from her thoughts? What does she mean with nothing? Or with connection? What specifically is not shared?

You may also notice that there's something behind this. How does she go from being motivated in the morning to her relationship? We can find out by following that energy, which is exactly what I did. *This present state of waking up in the morning is a result, not a cause.* We dived deeper into the cause and focus on the relationship with her life partner. One of the contexts in which her relationship problem arises, is when her partner doesn't do marketing activities for his own business and therefore he is not getting any new clients. This is just one example of where he does not take initiative.

As we explored this further, her way of responding in contexts like this developed from being in a convincer mode to alternating passiveness and anger. As time evolved, she steeled herself from disappointment by disconnecting. During the first few years of their relationship, when he wouldn't take initiative, she would take initiative herself and then talk about it with him in order to get him to take action next time (the convincer phase). This led to disappointment after disappointment. It also created the opposite effect with her partner.

Eventually she stopped talking about the things she wanted him to take initiative in, operating from a state of "indifference", and waited until he would start a conversation with her. This would work for a period of time, but she still held on to expectations, and eventually she would ask a question about it. This usually led to an explosion of anger on her part.

And guess what, it created more of the opposite effect with her partner! That's one of the confrontations I made to her.

Having done this long enough, she turned to passiveness and had steeled herself from disappointment. The act of steeling herself had turned into depression and loss of joy in life.

All of the information above is part of Phase I – Building The Story. In the beginning of the conversation I am getting the "lay of the land". Basically, I put the stories that she shares with me on a timeline and look at where the problem began.

By getting the lay of the land, we were able to detect the pattern that started all of this: trying to convince the other person of her needs in the hopes that they will meet it. Then she'd give up, and hide her sadness behind indifference (steeling herself). Even though the convincing didn't work – it led to disappointment instead – she would end up having hope again and continue to try and convince.

I asked her: "How many times do you think you need to express a need before the other person listens to it?"

It's a confrontational question, meant to build awareness over the reality that someone is not meeting her needs as well as ownership for the fact that she continues to cling to the hope or expectation.

At this moment, she sighs deeply. And answers: "Well, just once. Or perhaps two times if the person didn't understand. But not a thousand times."

Now we are building up the away from motivation that part of Phase IV – Setting The Outcome. The attempts at convincing her partner aren't actually working for her. For one, it is very exhausting, and there is a lot of sadness behind it. Yet it does have some payoff because otherwise she wouldn't be doing it. I needed to help her get to a place where she could make a better choice for herself and the energy was there to dive into that.

So I asked her: "What if you continue this for another 5 or 10 years?"

That's almost unbearable to think of. I just can't.

She shares that she is already at a point where she doesn't like being on this earth anymore, and speaks of wanting to go "home" (by which she means going back to where she came to this earth from). It would be a waste of her time, of her life. And there is a lot of disappointment in the fact that she let it go on for this long.

It didn't take much to build up the away from motivation. In fact, it was there all along, but it was directed in a less than productive way. The tears indicated that this was an important statement for her, so I asked her:

"Is that one of the steps that we need to work on, to grieve the past? To grieve the time that you've lost?"

Yes. And also to deal with the anger.

"Tell me more about the anger."

Well, I get angry when people don't give me what I want. But I suppress it and then start to try and convince.

Right here we have just jumped from Phase IV to Phase III. As we move along in the coaching session, I will identify with my client the steps that she needs to take in order to get to her outcome. At this point we don't know yet whether she can do that for herself or not. We have just identified the step.

We also got a little more information about her present state. We don't know much about the desired state yet. So I inquired about that.

"What do you want to feel instead?"

Empowered. Free. Independent. I want to be able to just focus on my own thing, and not be so focused on what I am not getting from others.

"What would you be focusing on specifically?"

On setting up my bed and breakfast. And doing the things that need to be done for that.

"What are those things?"

Well, I need to make a website, make sure that the rooms are set up, take care of Facebook and booking.com. So in the morning I want to wake up energized and motivated.

"And to do that, you need to be able to focus on your own thing, even when your needs aren't being met and your partner is not doing what you expect him to do?"

Yes.

"OK. And the state you want to be in is empowered, free and independent? *(Yes)* And how will that affect your relationship with your partner?

I don't know yet. But that's not what I want to focus on right now. I want to focus on me. Right now we have to live together because we have a big mortgage and neither of us can afford to move. That's a financial reality I am dealing with. Focusing on myself means that I can get out of that reality. (Here she gives a clue about her big "why")

"OK, and what does empowered, free and independent feel like?"

Free. I'll feel responsible for my own needs and put those first. I'll be acknowledging myself.

"And how would you do that in regards to your partner not hearing your needs and not taking initiative?"

I won't be focused on that. That's his stuff. I will focus on the things that are mine.

"OK, so just to recap, you want to be free, independent and empowered so that you will be able to focus on building your bed and breakfast. This means that you will create a different financial reality for yourself."

Yes.

"If you have that, how will you then be able respond to your partner when he doesn't take initiative on something?"

With acceptance.

"Right. Earlier you mentioned that you would get to a place of indifference. How is acceptance different from indifference?"

Yes, I think that's an important distinction to make. Because indifference is not really acceptance.

"From what I gather, the indifference is a way to hide the sadness and the anger?"

Yes.

"I wonder whether there's something else in addition to acceptance that we need to focus on. When you accept, you are still not getting what you want and need in your relationship. You said earlier that you feel anger. Could it be that you need to express that anger a different way? That it acts as a signal to you that a value is being violated, that you have a "no"?"

(As a coach, this is where I brought in some training (explaining that anger is an emotion and that it is informing her). In my years of building up experience, I can make an estimation of what my client might need that she cannot see for herself. Mere acceptance does not solve the fact that the relationship is not how she wants it to be. So the question that I have in the back of my mind is how she wants to deal with that so that she can truly acknowledge herself. This has a lot to do with boundaries and anger is an emotion that let's her know about her boundary. A boundary is closely related to your values, because it's essentially the difference between saying yes to what you allow in and no to what you don't allow in.)

Right, yes, that's true. So I need to see it as a signal so that I can say "This is not what I want," accept that and then move on. Ahh, ok, yes, and that's when the emptiness comes.

Up until this point she hadn't talked about emptiness. The way in which she said it (both in the words she chose and the tonality of her voice) let me know that this was something important. I don't know what she means with emptiness at this point, we will find that out later in the conversation. In my mind, I'm parking it AND I highlight it as something important.

Right now I am still on phase III, figuring out what we need to do to get to the desired state: Hmmm, ok! So we are getting an even clearer picture of how this works! And we will work on the emptiness, along with acceptance and building a different relationship to the emotion of anger so you can let it inform you.

"If we work on all of those, will that allow you to stay empowered, independent and free?"

Yes.

"And does that allow you to focus on your own things?"

Yes.

"OK, great."

We've now identified that for this part of her outcome, we will be working on the following:

* Grieving
* Acceptance (of her behavior in the past and of her partner's thinking styles)
* A different way to relating to feelings of anger
* Dealing with emptiness that comes from acceptance

We can then work on prioritizing this list by determining whether she can do it for herself or whether it's something we need to work on together (Phase III). We ended up identifying the acceptance, anger and emptiness as what we need to work on together.

In addition to waking up energized and motivated in the morning, focusing on her own things also meant sitting down and getting her website online. This was still something to explore in more depth.

Susan had a fear to get started, which led to procrastination. The mere thought of working on the website felt exhausting. It's important to note here that there are two distinct present states to separate. There is the moment that she *thinks* of working on her website and then there is the state of actually sitting down and doing the writing.

When we put the present states on a timeline, it's usually the first one that you need to focus on, because that's where the problem starts. However, it's up to your client to decide which one to go for.

As she thinks of writing the text, she sees all the different things that need to be in the text (all the things there are to see and do in the area, what you can have for breakfast, the photos that need to be in it, a description of the house and rooms). All those elements are jumbled together right in front of her in her mind's eye. She then wonders: "Is it not too much? Am I forgetting something?"

Her mind then goes to "What will others think of this? Shouldn't I be doing something else? It's not good enough (the writing)." *(Remember, she hasn't written anything yet.)* And: "You shouldn't think so much of yourself. You're not allowed to do this: who do you think you are?"

This is when she brings in her parents as references and examples of when they told her "there she goes again, she always has to be different", to which she drew the conclusion that she is an outcast. And with going for this dream of a bed and breakfast: she's the odd one out **again.**

Just a quick Detection and Analysis (Phase II) on this, Susan is operating from a strong external reference, using toxic reference experiences that are tied to her identity, which she subsequently tabooed. She is also predicting the future (prophesying).

This is how I presented this to her, after feeding back the structure of how she has created her present state: "It sounds like you are using a reference experience (your parents) that is not bringing forth your best and that you are using an external reference to decide your value?"

(I'd like to point out here that I have already provided my client with a list of cognitive distortions and thinking styles, explaining what they are and how they effect us. And I have shared with her that I will be listening for them and feeding it back to her.)

In addition, we uncovered that she overwhelms herself with too many options, and has a hard time procedurizing (everything is jumbled together right now). So now we have this information, we looked at what we need to focus on (Phase III). But first, what did she want to feel instead?

I want to have clarity about what I want to write, sit down and just write it.

Of course, she is not telling me what she feels. However, it is important information that we also need to know. It's a great way to get her into the desired state: "So let's say that you have clarity about what you want to write, what state are you in?"

Confidence.

I inquired about what confidence would feel like and what she would be seeing. She shared a reference experience with me of when she worked a journalist. After an interview, she'd sit down and know exactly what to write. We explored what she saw and felt in that situation, so that we can map it over. (Mapping it over means that we take the structure of how she gets into a state of confidence when she was a journalist, and apply it to the context of thinking of writing her website)

It turned out that she had everything organized in her mind. Visually, she'd see the bullet points of what she wants to write down. We translated that to sitting down to write the website, and in the desired state she sees the website right in front of her and can see what information goes where and what pictures go with it. That prompts her to "just start writing," like she used to do when writing articles for the newspaper.

As you might have noticed, there is a difference in her ability to procedurize and visualize. While initially those might have seemed to be easy fixes, this is not what we ended up having to work on in the coaching. Even though she experiences an inability to create structure, she is very capable of it. So the change power is somewhere else.

That's exactly what we grabbed hold of. The reference experience in combination with external referencing and over-identifying were the real culprits here. We had to work on changing those.

Now we had a whole list of things to work on:
  * Acceptance
  * Different relationship with anger
  * Emptiness
  * External reference experience / over-identifying

At the end of the second session, where we finished up the outcome statement and went to phase IV, Getting The Outcome. I asked her about the reference experience in relation to writing for her website. Funnily enough, it turned out that the solution was an easier fix that we had thought.

I asked her a testing question to see what we needed to work on. The picture of the reference experience was really a movie that she was playing right in front of her. "What happens if you put that movie behind you? Does that make a difference?"

It was silent for a moment, and then she said: "I had never thought of doing that!" She took this in the coming weeks after the coaching session, and it was the difference that she needed to be able to move into action.

That's the power of getting to where the leverage point is!

There was still more work to do though.

When we starting doing the change work for wanting to focus on her own thing, and began with the acceptance that others may not give her what she want or acknowledge her, that sense of emptiness popped up again. It turned out that this emptiness is what she was trying to avoid all this time and the reason for continuing to try and convince. *She was afraid of the emptiness.*

I asked her what she believes about the emptiness.

It's loneliness. It see it as having to start all over at my age (she's 65+).

By doing some quality control on the meanings she had given the space around her (that she had labeled as emptiness), she realized that thinking about it in this way was depressing. She wanted something else. (Phase IV)

"What else could it mean that would serve you better?"

It could also mean possibilities. That there's space for possibilities. And that I can honor my own values and wishes in that space.

"And what would that lead to?"

Self recognition. My relationship with myself is the most important one.

"How true is that for you?"

Oh, that's very true!

"If you were to see the space in this way, what would be important to you about that? "

(I'm sure you've already guessed it, but I just moved to Phase IV again.)

Then I can enjoy the things that I am doing.

"And what is important about that?"

Then I can connect and enjoy the people that surround me.

"What would that open up for you?"

I'd be happy in my own skin.

"And that's important to you?"

Yes. It's very important.

"Are you able to keep it that way?"

Yes.

"And how does this relate to your anger? Do we still need to work on that?"

Actually, no, I feel that with the acceptance and the possibilities, I will still know that this is not what I want but I don't have to fight for having my needs met. So the anger doesn't get as strong.

At the time of writing this book, she has put her bed and breakfast website online and within 1 week she is fully booked two months out. She said that she is tired (physically), but that she feels energized and comfortable in her own skin.

When I inquired how she is doing with her partner, she said that the other day she asked him how he was doing with his own business. He started expressing how he isn't taking action because he feels insecure and she shared that she was able to take herself out of the conversation and not let his feelings "drag her down". This way, she could maintain her focus on what is working for her and she placed responsibility for changing (or not changing) the insecurity to get different results in his business, with her partner.

Interestingly, her partner is now taking more responsibility and also has more energy. There is more connection and togetherness in the relationship. It could have gone a different way, too, at which point we might have needed to focus on how to

deal with that. Often, though, when one part of a system changes, it affects the entire system.

We ended up doing four sessions together.

Henry's Story

Henry came to me because he wanted to do executive coaching. He had been working as an HR manager most of his life and was now an internal coach, mostly working with mid-level managers.

Every month he would meet with the 5 directors of the company. He had been feeling tense and anxious every time he got called upon to meet with them. It's a feeling he had known very well since childhood, describing his father as overbearing and lacking in empathy. In his mind, he had generalized his dad's behavior to include people who are higher up in the hierarchy.

With wanting to transition into his own business, this was really something that got in the way. So he asked me to coach him on it.

In the present state, he feels anxious and tense. He feels this in the back of his neck, as the muscles tense up. And his stomach starts rumbling. His mind goes to "I'm not capable, I'm not valuable." This, then, leads to "I'm going into the unknown, and those people (the directors) will see that I am unable to do what they want me to do."

I then asked Henry: "Who are those people?"

The directors. They are not at the same level as me.

This was a cue for me to inquire about his social panorama (Lucas Derks), because he indicates that there is something important there by stating that they are not at the same level.

"In your mental space, where have you placed them?"

On top of my head.

(I joked with him that I understood where his tension headaches came from and why he feels such tension in his neck. We got a good chuckle out of that. This helps to not take the situation and the frames too seriously)

All of this led us to the following frames: "They are judges who will punish me. I don't want to live through that, because it makes me suffer. They won't see my beauty, they'll only see what I do wrong. That are business people, and they only see what they need done, not the employees. It's like the sword of Damocles hanging over me.

By this time, I had a pretty good idea of what was going on for Henry and how he created his anxiety and stress. We then moved to Phase II – Detection And Analysis. I started by giving him feedback on what I heard him say. One of his values is to be seen as a human being. He also does not want suffer. He had told me earlier that this tension was affecting his health, because he often had tension headaches.

So I asked him: "I am hearing you say that you don't want to suffer, but it sounds like you are already suffering by the way you are thinking and feeling about meeting with these directors?" This gave him the awareness that he was, in fact, *punishing and judging himself*. The directors weren't even involved.

I then went on to ask him about another incongruency (at least, that is how I perceived it, I told him to let me know if I was wrong). He wanted to be seen for who he was, not just as an employee who might make a mistake. By thinking and feeling this way, was he seeing the directors as human beings? Was he doing the very thing he did not want the directors to do to him?

He shared that they had given him permission to temporarily work part-time so he could take after his father. *And he realized that he was not only judging himself, but the directors as well.*

This is exactly what we want in Phase II of the Quantum Leap. We are building awareness so we can figure out what to change. And that can only happen when there is a sense of ownership. Henry was, in a way, blaming. In his mind he had placed the "fault" with others, even though these were his own meanings. I needed to make him aware of that.

Now we know that Henry, in this situation, is experiencing a limiting use of semantic space (his directors are on top of his head), he is judging himself and others, he is using an external reference for how he feels (something the directors do or say, can make him suffer), and he is predicting the future (they will see that I am unable to do what they want me to do and will punish me for it.) And lastly, we identified he is confusing human being with human doing, and he said: "I need to beef up my sense of beauty and value of myself".

Moving into Phase III, I started checking with him what we needed to work on. Starting with changing the position of the directors: "If the directors weren't on top of your head, where would they be?"

They would be at waist height. Then a silence followed. *Well, I realize that then I want to dominate.*

"Is that ecological for you?"

No, it's not, I want to be on equal terms.

"So where would you place them, if they were on equal terms with you?"

To my right, at shoulder height. And they would be at a normal distance. They don't have to be far away. (Here you could inquire about what normal means, how far that actually is.)

"Let's say that you have the directors to your right, at shoulder height, at just the right distance, would that allow you to feel confident when you are being called upon a meeting with any of the directors?" (He had mentioned in the beginning of our conversation that his desired state was confidence)

Well, if we put it on a scale, my anxiety would go from a 9 to an 8.

This is not a big difference, so now we know that this is not where the change power is.

"Alright, then let's check to see what happens when you move from externally referenced to internally referenced. What if you had an inner knowing that you are a beautiful human being who has value, regardless of what any of the directors say. What difference would that make?"

That would bring the anxiety down to a 5.

So we know that makes a difference, but it's still not where we want it to be. We added in the releasing of judgment of self, and of others, and that made it better still. However, Henry had a hard time imagining his own sense of beauty and value. So this was definitely something we needed to work on together. At this point, we don't know how yet, because we are just planning out what we will be working on over the course of the next sessions.

Now I moved back to Phase I – The Strategy Process, to get more information on the desired state. I knew he wanted to feel confident. But what would that feel like, sound like, what would he be doing? He mentioned confidence and that he wanted to feel relaxed.

"What would be different in your body, when you feel confidence and you are relaxed?"

My neck muscles would feel relaxed and I would just focus on the things I know how to do. I'd be honest about the things I don't yet know how to do.

Here Henry gave some of the answer for the VAK (visual, auditory, kinesthetic), and then he shared where his focus would be and what he would be doing. So we are starting to piece together the strategy process of the desired state.

"OK, you are able to concentrate on the things you are able to do. What will allow you to do that?"

By accepting that I will always be a work in progress.

"How much acceptance do you have for that right now?"

Oh, that's growing as we speak. It's about a level 6 right now.

"And how much would you like it to be?"

At a level 8 or 9.

"Are you able to do that yourself?"

Yes, if I have the self value, then that comes naturally.

"OK, so we don't need to work on that as a separate issue?"

No, I don't think so.

(We took a little detour here to Phase III, getting more information on the How)

"Let's get back to some of the beliefs that will support you in this new state. If you are able to concentrate on what you are able to do, accepting that you will always be a work in progress, how will you show up differently when you are called to meet with one of the directors (bringing it back to the context)?"

Well, I'll be able to evaluate myself freely. They have a business, and that comes with certain needs. And I just need to check if I can meet those needs. And then I can be honest about it to them.

"Who do they become?"

I can see them like friends. We might have different philosophies on life (or not), and if that's the case we can part ways.

"And what would that give you?"

Freedom. Real freedom.

"And would you like that?"

Yes!

This was a natural place to move into the next phase, Phase IV, Setting The Outcome. First, I asked a few more questions about his motivation towards the new state. He mentioned the book "Will The Real Me Please Stand Up," stating that he would be able to reach his full potential by making this change.

And that he will be able to be his true self, which leads to the freedom he spoke of earlier.

We also looked at the away from motivation. We already had some information on that. The fact that he regularly has tension headaches. So I asked him how else it is affecting him. Always feeling tired and having to make an effort to have a social life means that he is not living his life to the fullest.

"It sounds like it's important for you to make this change."

Oh, yes, it really is.

"And in order to create this change, we need to work on beefing up your sense of beauty and value of yourself, release your judgment of yourself and others, and separate human being from human doing, so you can accept that you will always be a work in progress. Is that correct?"

Yes.

"And you will know that you have your outcome when you are able to feel relaxed, have your neck muscles relaxed, are able to evaluate whether you are able to meet the needs of the directors and honestly state when you cannot deliver when you are called in for a meeting? Are you going to do that?"

Yes, definitely.

"OK, great. So next time we will start with making the first change. What would be the most impactful for you?"

The sense of beauty and value of myself, that I can fully see that.

"Awesome. We will start there then."

For the second session I checked in how Henry had done since last time we spoke. He shared that what we had discussed had been on his mind, and that he realized it would take some work to make the change.

Then I asked him about the outcome of today's session, referring back to what we had discussed in our first one: "Given that we have 1 hour together today, what is the most important item to work on out of what we have identified last session: the releasing of judgment, the internal referencing, and boosting your sense of value. It could also be something else that you have discovered since we last spoke."

The external referencing is of high importance and for me I would believe that goes together with how I value myself. Now my value is based on external referencing. So this is what I see and for sure I want to work on it and eventually make it something of the past.

So the outcome of today's session becomes internal valuing. Henry also mentioned that there are two separate triggers. His feeling is first triggered the moment that he wakes up. When he gets the phone call to meet with the directors, the feeling intensifies. This is important information to know, because we can test whether there has been a change in both situations.

I asked Henry how he values himself right now. Or rather, how he is not valuing himself right now. He said that he didn't know how to value himself. He knows that his value is not zero, but he would scale it around a two. At this point I want to know how he does that, valuing himself at a level two.

Henry went on to say that he knew that he has value. If you were to say to him that he doesn't have value, deep down he would feel that it's not true. It seemed that he knew that, but he didn't *feel* it. I asked him what he felt instead, and he replied with *'emptiness that wants to be filled'*.

The fact that he told me that he didn't know how to value himself, prompted me to dive deeper into his strategy for valuing something. What we discovered, was that he did have times that he valued himself, *on the condition that he had done something useful.*

This is where I do more of Phase II Detection and Analysis, and I explained to him that value is something unconditional. It's not about anything you say, do or think. And that it seemed to me that he was basing his value on exactly those things. Gathering more information about the present state, Henry mentioned that this had something to do in relating to others (locking down the context). When he is by himself, he knows and feels his value.

This is great, because then we know he can, in fact, value himself and feel it. That's not what we have to work on. There's something else that we have to yet find. So now we can map out the strategy process even more, and when he thinks of valuing himself in relation to others, he sees himself being criticized.

"Where did you learn that?"

I think that has something to do with my childhood, I never really felt loved. I never heard my mother or my father telling me I love you.

Henry drew the conclusion from never hearing his parents say "I love you", that he wasn't valuable. Again, here we worked on the awareness that it was, in fact, his conclusion. And I asked him: "Do you realize that you are NOT what other people say to you?" His identity and how he values himself was based on something that happened in the past, something that wasn't said to him. Once he saw that, he wanted to learn how to grow as a result of it, so he can feel more fully alive.

"So, Henry, on a scale from zero to ten how much do you realize that that says nothing about who you are as a person that it is just something that happened to you in your life."

I feel that what you said is really precious, can you repeat it?

"So on a scale from zero to ten how, much do you realize that even that fact that you did not hear I love you from your parents, says nothing about who you are as a person?"

You are quite right and in fact let me tell you my feeling I am really getting emotional right now when you say that, even weeping because what you are saying is that I have not come across that before and you are quite right.

"Yes, so just sit with that realization for a moment, knowing that it is true and allow whatever emotions is there to come up."

... (silence)

"So now Henry that you realize that you are not your past or what happened to you what awareness does that bring for you and what does the bursting of the bubble bring for you?"

I hear the words work in progress and it is as if now the work in progress which have been so far stagnant is coming back to life.

"Okay, and what happens to your sense of value that you are valuable just by being you even in the company of others."

It is as if you have a new treasure in your hand and you now get hold of it and it is so important that now you want to travel with it in your head.

The rest of the session we worked on getting Henry to be able to "travel with it in his head", and body. What this meant to Henry was that it would be a solid belief.

For our third session, I first checked in with Henry how things went after the last time we spoke. "I didn't do it as I would have liked. At first, I had a picture of big rough diamond in my hands, like the treasure I spoke of. This image was quite appealing to me." He mentioned that as a result, in the first week he could feel this new sense of "you are not your past or what people have labelled you in the past," very strongly and it affected the way that he approached his work. He felt this feeling of beauty of himself.

And then it faded away.

When he had the director's meeting the day before our meeting, there was some struggle. He did not at that time recall the insights from the coaching. He had not looked at his notes to be able to practice the state.

You are not what happened to you. That is still something that is really helpful. But I will be honest that when I needed to use it, I had forgotten about it.

"When you did remember it, how was that different from when you forgot about it?"

When I forgot about it, it's as if I was in the dark and you're looking for any clue that can guide you. Still, it didn't disturb me. I just told myself that this is a normal process. Even if I was in the darkness, I could be calm about that. Yet I would have liked to have been able to use it. It gives you something on which to build up your thinking. Instead of your thinking going in any direction or going astray.

I wanted to do some testing here to see what might be getting in the way of Henry remembering (feeling) the statement: "This sentence, on a scale from 0-10, how much do you understand this statement of 'You are not what happened to you in the past?'"

The understanding is very clear. I might even say an 8 or 9 out of a 10. It's as if I need to digest it and I need now for it to show up in my body, in my life.

"So your understanding is really high. How much do you feel it in your body?"

Yeah, that's low.

"Would it help to feel it in your body?"

Yes, I believe it is something that helps me not just to understand it but to make it come to life.

But there was something else that was getting in the way. He believed that change was not possible. Adopting a new way of thinking which is much more effective in his life seemed like something that was simply not do-able, and this was a big part of what was creating the struggle. He also said that he didn't know how to go about making that change.

So those were two things that we needed to work on. The fact that he didn't believe he can change and the fact that he didn't know how to go about making the change (to feel the new belief).

"If we were to change that, and get that out of your system, and bring into your feeling the notion that you are not what happened to you in your past. And you really feel it in your body, so that your unconscious mind can start operating in that way, would that make a difference for you?"

What you have just mentioned, I felt an insight. For sure I have been trying to understand that notion, but I have not been trying to feel it. There have been many things working in my mind, but not really feeling it. What is the feeling that comes out of that? I thank you, because this brings me an awareness: I was not trying to feel.

"Ahhh, ok, that makes sense. So is that what we need to work on: for you to feel it?"

Yes, Femke.

We ended up deciding on going through the Mind-To-Muscle Pattern, on how to bring an understanding into the body. You can find the pattern under Part VI -- Resources

Here's how we ended that process:

"Bringing this decision and this feeling that comes with it, into a situation where you are meeting with directors or coaching an executive, what difference does that make for you?"

I have an ally. It's as if you are your own best friend this way.

"Does this allow you to make mistakes and to continue to improve?"

Yes, I would be laughing about the mistakes.

"And have you decided to keep this?"

Yes, definitely.

Starting session four: "How have you been? I saw you've been working with some resources?"

Yes, I sent you some of the things that were useful for me.

During the weekend I took it very seriously because I wanted to meditate on understanding and at the same time feeling it. It seems to me that this is a practice that I must get into every day for 15 minutes. It is not so obvious for me because I've always been on the understanding side and keeping the feeling completely separated from it. Now I try to be aware what is going on in myself when I say to myself: You are not what happened to you. Now I am taking note of what is inside of the feeling.

"How much are you feeling this "You are not your past"?"

Well, in fact, I took this and during the week something popped up in my mind: As a coach and coachee I am well aware that my present state is because of certain beliefs that I have. And something which I have been using, which in fact I felt it quite strong, was the phrase: "No, no nonsense!"

Each time that I went into the pattern of thinking that I am not good enough, I am not valuable, now the phrase pops up: "No, no nonsense!" I noted it on my computer, and when I say this, what I feel is that I am taking myself seriously. I am loving and valuing myself.

"Nice. So that is one way of valuing yourself?"

Yes, and I found that in various instances where the erroneous beliefs come into play, I state this phrase and it helps me to pick up myself and not simply act out on feelings which I consider to be negative.

"And when you talk about negative, what is negative about them?"

Well, for instance this morning I was in a meeting with different HR managers and at a certain point I wanted to voice my opinion. Then came the thought: "You are going to make a fool of yourself." I went back to this phrase, and it helped me to tackle the situation and just go for it.

"Nice. So you are not feeding it. You're actually cutting it off."

Yeah. Yeah.

"You say that you went for it. What was your experience then?"

What I experienced, I gave myself the opportunity to be free. With your help, I really saw how negative beliefs hinder you from being yourself and growing as a human being.

"Now when you think of going into a meeting with executives, and you have the resource of saying no and valuing yourself, how does that change the meeting?"

It helps me to be resourceful. I've been listening to all the coaching sessions I had with you during the weekend and took notes.

"What it sounds like to me is that you can say no, so that it can make place for the new belief. It may be that you need to say no first, so that you can bring the other in. So it sounds like you've made a huge step in the right direction?"

Yes.

"What else is it that you need? What do you need to work on in this session that would make a difference for you?"

I think I just need to continue to practice this.

"Is there any form of resistance left from bringing it into your body?"

No. This really has made a tremendous difference. And with practice I know I can get rid of the negative thoughts altogether. I doesn't have a hold over me anymore.

Henry ended up emailing me a few weeks after our last session. He shared that he freed himself from perpetual anxiety in relation to meeting with executives or even in social settings. He had tried many things, even thought that it was impossible to change it since he has been walking around with it for 35 years. It took us four sessions to transform his pattern.

Troubleshooting Your Sessions

During one of my sessions with Henry, the change we had worked on the previous session had not solidified as he would have liked. He actually had a belief that change was not possible for him, because he had tried so many things and he had been struggling with this for about 35 years.

It's not uncommon that change doesn't stick. And that's ok. It just lets you know that there's something that is getting in the way. I've created a short list of what those things might be.

Not enough motivation

The pain of the present situation may not be strong enough. At least not as strong as the fear of changing. Or as strong as the desire for a different outcome.

Hasn't made a decision

Your client's strategy for making decisions might not be a successful one. Even though the motivational energy is there, they might not be focusing on it because the commitment has not been made. This might mean that they aren't practicing the new states, which is imperative for implementing change. Your client may also have a strong external reference for decision making, so they are easily swayed by those around them. Alternatively, there may be some objections that are getting in the way and that have not been addressed yet. When you notice there is no follow through on the insights from the coaching sessions, this is one aspect you can check with your client.

Didn't grab hold of the leverage point

It can be as simple as not having identified the highest frame yet. This means you'll have to dive in deeper and ask more meta-questions to bring to light the frames that are the driving force behind the state.

Your client is emotionalizing

When your client takes their emotions for gospel, they will have a hard time stepping back from it when the emotion hits. They'll feel like they won't have a choice but to act on their emotions.

Your client thinks in all-or-nothing terms about change

Let's say you've had a great session. Your client got some great insights, you have identified some steps to take to solidify the change. He goes out and gives it a first try. But it doesn't go as he had expected. So he concludes: Well, this didn't work. And gives up.

Thinking in all-or-nothing terms about change stops your client from persevering and giving it a solid effort. They will give up after one try. When this happens, you might need to work on this cognitive distortion.

Doesn't truly believe change can happen

This is a belief that can really get in the way of allow for change to occur. This is especially the case when your client has tried different things to solve their problem in the past, and where they did not get the resolution they were after. They feel that the change is out of their power / control.

Preference for pondering

Your client may be addicted to a-ha moments. Yes, that's right, getting insights and light-bulb moments may be so exciting to your client, that all they want is to read some more about it, or philosophize just a little longer. Their focus in not on taking action, and nothing really changes.

Preference for taking action

If your client has a preference for taking action, you might be "fooled" into thinking that your client is thinking of solutions during the coaching session. However, those solutions are focused on dealing with the symptoms and not with the actual cause. Having a preference for taking action means that your client may not have the patience to reflect. On the outside it seems that you're "getting shit done", but it won't create lasting change.

Overly optimistic

The decisions your client makes during coaching, will have an affect on others in their lives. In interacting with others, some things will be out of your client's control. This is why you want to help your client make an informed decision about the change they are after. What are the possible consequences of this change in other areas in their lives?

If your client is overly optimistic, they'll have a hard time seeing any negative consequences. To give you an example, one of my colleagues had a client who had met someone while he was still married. He had been afraid of approaching his wife about a divorce and so he sought out coaching. He was convinced that his wife would be ok with a divorce, so they did not work through alternative scenarios. It came as a huge shock to him that she ended up wanting to fight for the marriage, and had no idea how to respond in that situation.

While this is an extreme example, it pays to help your client go through different scenarios of what might happen so that they can be prepared for whatever comes their way.

Part IV Focus Points

* Pre-framing saves you a lot of time during the coaching and gets you greater results
* Sometimes it's not possible to get those states right away and do the grounding of the outcome. Getting a lay of the land and time lining your client's stories will help you identify which states to work with.
* The Quantum Leap is a model. It's a simplified version of reality. This means that there are times where you can't follow the model to a t. If you try to make your client fit the system, you'll lose rapport. Use the system as a guideline, not as a rigid set of rules.
* If your client doesn't know how to answer certain questions, know that you can get other pieces of information first and then come back to the part of the QL system where there are still information gaps.
* Your client will share information without you having asked the question. Listen for this information to fill in the QL template and use it to build the client's story.

{ Part V }

The Coaching Skills

Ken Blanchard is often credited for the quote "Feedback is the food for champions." He first heard that phrase from his formed colleague Rick Tate. Explaining it in sports terms, he asked Ken: "Can you imagine training for the Olympics with no on telling you how fast you ran or how high you jumped?"

That idea seems crazy. So how could you expect to master the art and science of coaching without getting feedback on how you are doing? Giving feedback on an intangible, such as a skill, is not an easy feat. It can't easily be measured, but that does not mean it is impossible.

Competency based testing is said to have its source with David McClelland in his 1973 paper "Testing for competence rather than for intelligence." After writing his piece, he was approached by several large organizations and he chose to work with the U.S. State department to improve their failing selection process. He identified competencies underpinned each competence with behavioral indicators.

L. Michael Hall further developed this into his Benchmarking model. What distinguishes the Benchmarking model is that it uses the NLP meta-model (the model for specificity) to get even more specific on the behavioral indicators. Essentially, when measuring a skill, you want to be able to know what you'd see and hear when witnessing a competency at play.

Using the process of benchmarking, we have identified 7 coaching skills that play a role in the Quantum Leap system.

There are 4 skills that you will use at any given time in a coaching session:
1. Questioning
2. Listening
3. Inducing States
4. Building Client Awareness

Image 25 Core skills of coaching

In addition, there are the skills that are specific for each phase of the Quantum Leap:

1. Strategy process
2. Detection and analysis
3. The how
4. Setting the outcome
5. Getting and testing the outcome

Questioning

"Because questions are intrinsically related to action, they spark and direct attention, perception, energy, and effort, and so are at the heart of the evolving forms that our lives assume. Creativity requires asking genuine questions, those to which an answer is not already known. Questions function as open-ended invitations to creativity, calling forth that which does not yet exist."

Marilee Goldberg

Your questions will direct your client's attention. They are your main tool that allows your client to understand their problem, gain awareness to get to choice point, and build the energy and motivation to make the decision for change. They then allow your client to move into action.

Types of Questions

Exploration Questions

These are open-ended questions to get your client to share more information about a certain topic. Although it's not an actual question, a great example of an exploration "question" is "Tell me more about...".

Other examples are:
- In what other situations does this happen?
- What happens when you find yourself in this situation?
- How is x related to y?

Clarity Questions

In order to understand what your client is talking about, you will need to ask clarity questions. These are the types of questions that help you gain clarity as to how someone is using a specific word or how they are using their words as symbols.

Without it, we'd need to fill in a lot of the details ourselves, which has a negative effect our coaching skills.

Let's say the topic of the coaching conversation is about love, then what specifically does your client mean with that word? Self love? Romantic love? And if it is self love, what specifically does that mean? The idea here is that you ask enough detailed questions so you can see and hear what your client is seeing and hearing when they refer to a certain word.

As such, you may need to ask this questions several times because initially your client gives synonyms rather than an explanation of the "process" of self love. "Self love means that when I make time to exercise 5 times a week," or "Self love means that I say no when I don't want to do something, without feeling guilty."

Clarity questions help you ground a conversation, so that you and your client know what you are talking about, and you are talking about the same thing.

The example above, is related to a tendency to use nominalizations: pseudo-nouns that hide processes and actions. It's one of the twelve distinctions Bandler and Grinder identified when they studied Virginia Satir, Fritz Perls, and Milton Erickson who seemed to have "magical" effects on their clients. Other examples of sentences where representational details are missing:

"I want to learn how to deal with difficult people in the work place."

What does "dealing with" look like? Who are the people that are difficult? In what way are they difficult, specifically?

"Life is unfair. I always end up drawing the short end of the stick."

What specifically are you referring to when you say "drawing the short end of the stick?" What do you mean with always? When specifically have you drawn the short end of the stick? How does this make life unfair?

"He makes me so angry."

Who is he? How is he making you angry? How do you do anger?

When we are gathering information from our client, we listen for any distortions, generalizations and deletions in what our client is saying so that we can ask questions that fill in the details. In Part V – Patterns and Processes you will be able to review the Meta-Model distinctions and the kinds of questions to ask to gather information from your client.

Meta-Questions

While clarity questions are questions that help your client "come back to their senses" (primary state), meta-questions help your client go inside and explore their thoughts, feelings, conclusions, understandings, beliefs in the back of their minds. It's the exploration of how your client relates to their primary state.

What state are you inducing with your meta-questions? And what information do you need form your client to induce the meta-states needed for creating and solidifying change?

There are three rules to remember when asking meta-questions.
1. Grounded

When asking a meta-question, you need to relate it to something specific. You are directing your client's attention to a meta-state through your meta-questions and the question is what you want that state to be in relation to.

"What do you believe about that?" will generate a different response than "What do you believe about your husband raising his voice."

2.   Relevant

The question is related to the outcome or any aspect of helping your client achieve their outcome. If not, you can gather a lot of information about their belief systems, but it won't actually add to the purpose of the conversation.

Your client, for example, might be talking about freedom. And you ask them "what do you believe about freedom?" Well, this might lead your client to go off on a tangent about all the different ideas he has about what freedom means to him. It's not relevant to the outcome of experiencing a sense of freedom in their relationship. To make it relevant, you can then ask: "What do you believe about freedom in the context of your relationship?" This is both an example of relevance as well as groundedness.

3.   Timely

A meta-question is most powerful when you ask the question at a time when your client's attention is "there". If they talk about something and you notice they get into state, ask your meta-questions sooner rather than later. If you wait several minutes, you lose the energy of the moment.

List of Meta-Questions

There are over a hundred ways to ask someone what their relationship is with either an external event or an internal thought or feeling. At times you will want to be very specific as to where you lead your client. For example, when you are helping them discover their big enough why, you ask questions that help them access the meta-state of importance or intention: "What is important to you about...? And why is that important to you? What positive difference will that make in your life?"

Some meta-questions are more "neutral" in that they do invite your client to go in and up, but without determining the specific meta-state it induces: "What do you believe about x" or "What meaning have you given y?" If at any time your client has a hard time answering a meta-question, you can simply ask another one.

Here is a short-list of common meta-questions you can ask.

Meaning
What meaning have you given this? What meanings are you holding in mind about this?

Belief
What do you believe about this? What belief do you have about this belief?

Frame / reference

What frame of reference do you use for this? How are you framing this experience? What reference experience do you have for this?

Understanding
What understandings do you have about this? What do you understand about this?

Permission / Allow
Do you have permission to experience this? Have you allowed yourself to think and feel in this way?

Thoughts
What do you think about this? What thoughts run in the back of your mind about this?

Appreciate
What do you appreciate about this experience? What can you appreciate about this?

Decision
Have you made a decision about this? What decision do you need to make about this?

Conclusion
What conclusions have you drawn about this? What new conclusion can you draw from this that serves you better?

Value
What values are behind this? What do you value about this?

Difference

What difference will this make in your life? How is x different with this new understanding?

Testing Questions

The purpose of asking this type of question, is to determine whether or not something is true for your client. It's a closed-ended question: They will need to go inside and check inside themselves whether the answer is yes or no. There are several instances in which you'd be asking this type of question.

Phase II – Detection and Analysis: When you go through the process of prioritization of what would make the biggest difference, you ask questions like: If you separated human being from human doing, so you can understand that you are not what you do, would you then be able to do your desired state?

Phase III – The How: In pinpointing what it is specifically that your client needs to be coached on, you ask questions like "Can you do that?", "Have you done that before?" or "Is this what we need to be working on?"

Phase IV – Setting The Outcome: In order to have your client make a decision, you will be challenging your client away from the present state. "Do you want to keep doing this?" or "Does this make your life a party?". Ultimately, you'll want to get a clear decision, which is also in the form of a testing question: "Are you fully committed to making this change?" and "Are you sure?"

Phase V – Getting And Testing The Outcome: As you create the change with your client, you will be testing to see whether you are on the right track and whether there are any objections that get in the way of keeping the change: "Does this help you feel calm about your anger?" and "Are there any objections to moving forward with this?"

As you can see, testing questions play a pivotal role in coaching and are asked throughout the conversation.

Checking Questions

Whereas a testing question is about establishing with your client whether something is true, a checking question is about you verifying your own understanding about what your client has shared so far. It could be that you see a relationship between two elements of the story, and you are making sure you understood this correctly: "Earlier in the conversation you spoke about x and now y comes up. Am I understanding it right that these are related?" This type of question is asked to make sure we are not mind-reading.

Lack of skill present:

Of course, the lack of questions would be the first indicator that the skill of questioning is not present. There are also a lot of questions you can ask that take away from the power of coaching.

Mind-reading

When you assume that you know what your client is talking about or what they need to do to get their outcome, without checking it with your client, the quality of your questions will be affected. You'll be more prone to ask leading or irrelevant questions.

Leading questions

A leading question takes your client into a direction that you decide, rather than letting your client lead the way. It can be as simple as asking a closed ended question: "Would you like to work on a or b?" This forces your client to make a decision on these two options, rather than leaving it open.

Irrelevant questions

These kinds of questions dive deeper into the content, rather than the structure. Often it's about satisfying our own curiosity and it's not related to the outcome in any way. "What is your cat's name? How long have you had him? Do you still spend a lot of time with your siblings?"

Questions For a Well-Formed Outcome (Using the Quantum Leap)

Coaching is, of course, about getting an outcome for your client. It makes sense, therefore, that we place a lot of emphasis on how to identify the best possible outcome and finding the "what behind the what". The process for creating a Well-Formed Outcome stems from Neuro-Linguistic Programming, and Dr. Michael Hall further developed this pattern.

In each phase of the Quantum Leap, you will be asking different types of questions. From exploration questions to meta-questions to testing questions, within each of the phases they will have a different purpose. And as you might have gathered already, going through the first four phases of the Quantum Leap **will lead you set an outcome with your client.**

A lot of those questions originated from the Well-formed Outcome pattern. But there were some key questions missing. Questions that make a difference in getting the leverage point. They are covered in the Quantum Leap phases.

Here is an overview of questions to ask for each of the different phases. In the toolkit that you can download as part of this book, you will find a printable version of the image you see below.

The Quantum Leap Coach System -- Overview of questions

Ecology: What consequences might this change have? (pro / con)
Is this change ok in all areas of your life?

Decision: Will you do this?
Outcome: Is this the outcome we are going for?
KPI: Is (KPI) how we will test that you have your outcome?

Detection and analysis:
I notice some all or nothing thinking going on. Do you recognize that?

Why not:
What will it cost you to keep doing this?
What will happen if you did this for another five years?

Why:
What is important about having this state?
What will that give you?
What difference will that make?

Beliefs:
What reference experience do you have for that?
What do you believe about x (trigger) that makes you feel (state)?

How:
What do you need to do?
Can you? Have you?
If you change (pattern D&A), will that allow you to do your desired state?

Beliefs:
What needs to be true to believe that?
What do you need to believe to feel (state)

VAK: What do you see / hear when you are in this state?

Trigger: Where, when and with whom specifically?

Behavior: what do you no longer want to be doing?

What do you want?
VAK: What will you see/hear/feel when you have that?

Behavior: What will you be able to do?

Context: Where, when and with whom does this state occur?

Image 26 The print book does not show the colors of the different phases. You can download a color version at https://www.thecoachmentor.org/ql-toolkit.

Phase I — Strategy Process

What?

What not?

Where?

When?

With whom?

What do you see / hear / feel now?

What will you see / hear / feel when you have that?

Phase II — Awareness, Detection, and Analysis

I notice some all-or-nothing thinking going on. Do you recognize that?

Are you aware that this is the third time you've used the word "never"?

Could it be that you are prophesying?

While Phase II places an emphasis on giving feedback and providing a mirror for your client, questions are still important here. You are asking testing questions to solidify the awareness of what is going on. This is a critical component of getting a well-formed outcome. Without the insight that comes from this phase, it will be hard for your client to ask the question "what do you need to work on to get to your outcome?" or "what do you need to do to get there?"

This is where you find where the change power is.

Phase III — Defining The How

What do you need to do to get there?

Is it in your power?

Can you do that?

Have you done that before?

What are the steps involved?

What resources do you need?

Are there any blocks to doing this?

Phase IV — Setting The Outcome

Motivation

Why is this important to you?

Why do you not want this? What is it costing you?

Ecology and Decision

Is it ecological for you?

What are the pros and cons of making this change?

What are the pros and cons of not making this change?

How do all the pros and cons weigh up against one another?

Key Performance Indicator

What will be the evidence that you've reached your outcome?

How will you monitor your progress on this?

Once you have all of that information, you are ready to get to phase V – Getting And Testing The Outcome.

Listening

You can't ask great questions without listening intently to what your client is communicating. And it takes more than just your ears to really listen. As a coach, you are using your eyes and your body as well.

In Neuro-Linguistic Programming we often speak about building rapport through matching. And while that is one effect of matching voice tone, tempo, body posture, etc., it's also a way to truly listen to what your client is communicating.

Let me give you an example. Years ago I attended a training on personal effectiveness. One of the exercises we did was about depth of listening. There were 4 people to go through the process.

One person would be the model, one person would be modeled after the first person, and two people would "mold" the second person.

The first person would think of a moment in time where they experienced a strong emotion, either positive or negative. In their mind, they'd choose a snapshot of that experience and show how they responded in that situation and freeze in that position.

The second person would have their back to the first person, so they wouldn't be able to see the emotion. And the two others would then shape them to match in posture, muscle tension, breath, facial expression, of the first person.

It took quite a while, standing there frozen in time, before the matching was done. The guy who was being matched to my experience, was very down to earth. He didn't have think this exercise would have any effect. After we went through the process of molding and shaping, he was supposed to stand there for a little bit and just feel.

He was then asked: What were you experiencing? He said he couldn't quite place it, because he hadn't felt anything like that in his life. It was as if he had to say goodbye to someone important, but that he didn't know how.

My eyes opened wide. He was so spot on, it was freaky.

The moment I had chosen, was the first time I saw my dad after he had died. I was nine. I never knew how I had felt in that moment, until he voiced it.

We were both in shock and in awe.

It was that moment that taught me the power of listening with our entire body. He, of course, had no context or situation to place it in, but he could feel the state. And that's an important place to be in for understanding your client. Questions help us gain a great understanding of our client's outcome, needs, limiting beliefs, etc. Listening helps us to know what question to ask next to uncover more parts of their story.

Matching voice / energy / tempo / key words / semantic gestures

To listen with our entire body, we match voice, energy, tempo, posture, and breath. In NLP you learn that through matching you can make your client feel heard, and that it builds rapport. At the same time, it gives you a feel of your client's state so you can check it against what you are talking about at the moment. Of course you can do this by calibrating to some extent, yet in making it a full-body experience you'll get more information.

We also match the semantic gestures. This allows us to become aware of the way our client is using their semantic space.

As we uncover the present and desired state, trying on what our client tells us is a way to know what information we have and what information is still missing.

When, for example, your client is using a specific gesture that he/she keeps repeating over and over, matching that gesture will make you aware that there is something going on there. You'd need to ask your client what it means, which you are more likely to do when you repeat the same gesture.

Key words

A key word is a word our client is using that is in some way, shape or form, related to the outcome they are after. As a coach, we use the exact same word rather than using our own terminology (paraphrasing).

We can recognize a key word by something they repeatedly say, or when they emphasize the word with their tone of voice or specific gesture.

It not only creates a disconnect with our client when we start using our own words, it also inhibits our ability to gather valuable information because we start making assumptions about what they mean when they are using a certain word.

When your client uses the term lack of confidence, and you change that into insecurity, there's a good chance that your client does not feel understood or heard. Asking "what specifically do you mean with insecurity?" when they've not actually used that word, takes them away from the images, thoughts, reference experiences, etc., that they had in mind when they were talking about their lack of confidence.

Encouragers

An encourager is either a physical or verbal indicator for the client to continue speaking and sharing. This can be a nod, ok's, yes's, hmmm's.

Silence

Maintaining a silence for 3 seconds or longer allows our client to sit and reflect at a deeper level. It gives them time to process and feel into their body. So often we are sharing stories, but we are not actually listening to what we are saying. Holding a silence invites us to listen to ourselves.

Lack of skill present:

Mind-reading

When we think we know what our client means and don't test that assumption, we are mind-reading. Instead of listening and asking questions, we build our own pictures and stories in our mind and assume they are our client's.

Advice giving

Giving advice, rather than helping our client find their own answers, takes away from the skills of listening and questioning.

Things not heard

In a situation where your client repeats something several times, indicating that it bears relevance to the outcome and you are not picking up on this, it's something that you haven't heard.

It could also be that the conversation goes to a different level (the what behind the what) and you continue to ask questions that are about the symptoms rather than the cause. For example, when your client says "I need a plan." and in inquiring into this your client says "Well, I know how to create my plan. It's just that I don't feel confident that I will take action on it." When you continue to focus on creating a plan, you have missed the fact that the conversation should be about the lack of confidence in taking action.

Chasing client's words

It's not uncommon for a client to share a story, and then jump to another story because something you ask reminds them of that other situation. It gets them off track from the outcome they had set with you. When you jump to that other story with that, without checking to see how the two are related (if at all) and whether this is getting closer to the core of what you need to work on in order to achieve the outcome, you are chasing your client's words. This often happens when you are not making a distinction between the different present or desired states that your client is talking about, or when you haven't grounded the conversation in a specific context and trigger.

Inducing States

He stepped out onto the stage while it was still dark. One. Two. Three. Then back. One. Two. Three. We couldn't see him, only hear his footsteps. The microphone in front on the stage picked them up clearly. One. Two. Three. And back. One. Two. Three.

For six years, those steps were all he could take. Captain Charlie Plumb, a graduate from the Naval Academy at Annapolis, flew the F-4 Phantom jet on 74 successful missions. On his 75th, five days before he was to return home, he was shot down, captured and imprisoned by the enemy. For 2,103 days he was a Prisoner of War. His cell was 8" by 8". Three steps took him from one wall to the other.

Though there's no contact with other prisoners, they find inventive ways to communicate through code. About 200 miles into his experience, Plumb is approached by Shumacher – another P.O.W. – through a metal wire that he put through a hole in the wall between their cells.

Lieutenant Commander Bob Shumacher: "How you doing, buddy?"

Ah, that was Charlie's cue, he had been looking for somebody to tell his sorrows, so he said: "I am doing terrible! For goodness sake, my President sent me over here, I get shot down. It's his beautiful little war, now look who's paying the price. And then some idiot mechanic put a faulty transmission in that airplane, something went wrong, it wasn't my fault! And get Congress over here, let them sit in this prison cell! I am going to rot away and die in here, help me!"

Bob: "You want to know your biggest problem?"

Charlie: "Oh man! You mean I got problems bigger than the ones I can see?"

Bob: "Sounds like you are suffering from a fairly common prison disease. Around here we call the disease Prison Thinking."

Charlie: "Prison thinking?"

Bob: "Roger, you think you are a prisoner."

Charlie: "Look at this, I am bleeding from four open wounds. I have four holes in my body where blood's running out. I've no medical care. I have boils all over my front, all over my back, I am down to 115 pounds, my sole possession in life is a rag that I've knotted around my waist to hide my nudity. I am rotting away in a communist prison camp, and now – to add insult to injury – they put me next to a positive thinker! But OK, tell me about this prison thinking stuff."

Bob: "Don't you see? When a fighter pilot is first blown out of the sky, (or a manager is rebuked one more time, or a sales person is turned down one more time, or a mother is having challenges with that unruly child one more time), what the first emotion for all of us? Oh God, why me?! This is so terrible, what can be worse than this? This event will never have any value. In fact, the best this can be is make it through this tough time and try to forget it. Emotion number two is 'hey, I didn't start this war, I didn't build this airplane, I am the victim!' I've no control over my destiny. Emotion number three: If it's not my fault, it has got to be somebody else's fault. Problem here is you start blaming other people for your problems, you give away control of your life."

Thinking you are a prisoner: That's what got prisoners killed. Why? Because they saw no way out, they felt **powerless** and either gave up or spent all their energy fighting their circumstances. In his presentations, Charlie Plumb draws parallels between his experience as a P.O.W. and the challenges of everyday life.

As you can probably tell, Charlie was really good at inducing himself in a state. In fact, we do this all the time with the stories we tell ourselves. The more powerful the visuals and realistic the sounds in our mind, the stronger the state is.

Our meanings and stories determine the way we see the world, and how we feel about it. When we habitually think a certain way, it becomes our attitude towards life, situations and people. That's when things get tricky. Since we are so deeply invested in our thoughts at that point, and we've identified with it, it becomes our truth. It feels true. And then it becomes our filter for understanding the world around us.

The truth is, however, that our understanding and beliefs are liable to error. We draw conclusions based on limited information, and many of our beliefs are formed at a young age where we have a limited vocabulary so things get distorted. And since many of our beliefs have been with us for a long time, they become our blind spots. Charlie Plumb only became aware of his attitude when someone made him aware of it. This awareness brought him to **choice point:** either stick with his attitude or choose a more empowering one. Without awareness, we are unable to choose our attitude.

Awareness is the first step towards choosing our attitude. The next step is to quality control our attitude and determine whether it empowers us or not. Does this serve me? Does it give me more freedom, joy, creativity, etc.? Or does it hurt me? Once we've made this **choice**, we can determine what would serve us better. What state of mind and emotion can I bring to this situation so I can be more effective?

Our ability to reflect – through awareness – is unique to human beings. It allows us to step back from our own thoughts and feelings (our state) and reflect upon those thoughts and feelings. This is when we can choose our thoughts and feelings ABOUT our thoughts and feelings. For example, we can feel angry at our own anger, but what if we felt calm about our own anger? Would that make a difference? It would, wouldn't it?

Here's how it works:

We are always in a state. We are never not in a state. As the sum of our thoughts and feelings and physique at a given point in time, our states are constantly changing. The quality of our state is determined by the quality of our thoughts and feelings, which in turn determines the quality of our day, our week, our month, etc.

A primary state is comprised of our thoughts and feelings about an external event. It does not stop there, though. We continue to have thoughts and feelings about our thoughts and feelings, and then have thoughts and feelings about those thoughts and feelings. This process goes so fast, that we aren't aware of it. In essence, we are bringing one state to another state. And since "meta" refers to a relationship or "aboutness", those thoughts and feelings about our thoughts and feelings are called meta-states.

We often think that external events trigger our states. Something made us angry or happy. What happens, though, is that the way we evaluate and interpret the event ultimately determines our state of mind. And since this happens inside of us, it is something that we can control. Victor Frankl, in his book "Man's Search for Meaning", wrote about his experience in a concentration camp and he said about it: "They can't make me hate them."

He described this as the ultimate freedom that cannot be taken from a man; His freedom to choose his responses.

State Induction In Coaching

Without state induction, there is no change.

So how do we use the notion that we have thoughts and feelings about our thoughts and feelings (meta-states) in coaching? Well, we can help our clients choose different thoughts and feelings (a different state) about their thoughts and feelings. When we choose something more empowering, we create a new experience for ourselves. And that means that we get access to different actions, and different responses, thereby going from where we are to where we want to be.

To solidify change, our client needs to go through several different states. **A few examples are states of awareness, motivation, decision, creativity, brainstorming, resource states, present and desired state.**

As you go through the Quantum Leap system with your client, you wouldn't nearly have the same impact in the conversation if you weren't inducing them into the different states.

Our questions induce states. The way we ask the questions, with our physiology, voice and gestures, will have an effect on the intensity of the state we induce. As will the timing of the question.

There are several principles of a state to take into account when using it in your coaching:

It needs to be grounded in a context and trigger

Inducing your client into a state, is easy. Just ask them to talk about an experience in detail, and they'll naturally go into state. If your client wants to experience joy, you can help them access that state in under a minute. However, the real test is whether they are able to access it in a situation where they need that state.

The way we ask questions will help us ground the state. When we ask meta-questions, for example, we can ask "You just said that when you are thinking of writing your website text, you think it's not good enough, what on earth are you doing, and that it's your parents' voices that you are hearing. What do you become aware of in regards to that?" This is different from just asking: "What do you now become aware of?" In both cases you are inducing the state of awareness. However, the question is whether the second question will get you the information you need, since it is not related to anything in particular.

Using sensory specifics allows a person to get into a state

When your client is able to see and hear in full color and surround sound the visual and auditory details that drive a specific state for them, the strong they'll be induced into that state. Without it, you can talk about the state, but there's no actual accessing of it. Asking for these details means that you can feed it back to them when needed.

Your voice and gestures need to be congruent with the state

Let's say you want to induce the state of excitement. Your tone of voice is monotone, no smile on your face, and you are slumped in your seat. How would you rate the likelihood that your client will access excitement?

I'd say it's slim to none.

As human beings we have a natural tendency to mimic the emotional expressions of others, and in many cases even feel the same feelings simply by exposure to them in social interactions. We can actively help our client access the state they want and need, by leading the way and accessing those states ourselves first.

The intensity of the state is important

Imagine your client struggling with intense anger (level 9) and you've identified with him that texturing it with calmness would make a difference for him. As you help him access a calm state, it's at a level 2. This won't have much of an effect on the high level anger that he feels. So we need to amp it up to a level 9 or 10 to be able to texture and transform the anger.

States are accessed through memory, imagination or physiology. In helping your client access a state, you can invite them to think of a memory where they felt that state strongly. You can also invite them to change their physiology or help them image a situation in which they'd have that state, such as stepping into someone's shoes who already has access to it.

Small referent experiences keep the state as clean as possible

When Max was asked to access the state of "No!", he took a referent experience of him saying no to his parents on something that they wanted him to do. As he accessed the state, it became clear that he had textured it with defensiveness, which indicates a power struggle. Yet, what we want when setting a boundary, is a neutral "No!" The coach had to help Max find a situation where he said "No!" without feeling threatened or that it won't be accepted.

It could be something like smoking a cigarette or getting crazy stupid drunk. Something you can easily say "No!" to. The same goes for other states that we want to help our client access and apply to a specific trigger or thought.

Building Client Awareness

Feeding back client's story (words)

To help our client hear themselves and gain awareness as to how they have created their present state or how they'd be doing their desired state, we need to feed back our client's story. This is more than just repeating what our client has just said. We show them how a trigger leads to an internal response of images, beliefs, layers of meanings, that drives the state and leads to a certain behavior. In drawing this picture, our client gains the necessary insights to play an active role in detecting and analyzing patterns in order to make an informed decision about what to change and whether to change.

Confronting and challenging

We confront our client on a blind spot, an incongruence, or when there is a need to hold them accountable on something they said they were going to do. We can do this through feeding back their words, and pointing out an inconsistency. Alternatively, our client may be saying something and their body language shows something entirely different.

Another way of confronting our client, is by showing that their way of thinking and feeling is creating the very thing they are trying to avoid, which is a common occurrence in coaching. We end up creating the very thing we are trying to avoid.

When we challenge our client, we invite them to step outside of their comfort zone. Perhaps they don't want to discuss something, yet that's exactly where they need to go in order to get the outcome they are after. Or they are afraid of doing something, and you challenge them to go ahead and do it regardless of the discomfort or fear. Perhaps by trying on the new behavior for a limited period of time, to see how it fits.

Listen for and feedback values

In sharing their stories, our clients leave clues for us on what is important in their lives. They may not be explicit about it, or even be aware about the values that drive their stories, but we can listen for them and feed it back tentatively: "It sounds like freedom is an important value for you."

Framing

There are several ways in which we use framing in a coaching conversation. We start with pre-framing what our client can expect.

Some examples of pre-frames are:
* I will be interrupting you from time to time, because I don't need a lot of content. Coaching is about process and the structure of our experience, and to make the most of our time together I will let you know when I have enough information.
* All emotions or thoughts that come up, are ok. I'd like you to feel free to share them.
* Coaching is not about me giving advice. I believe you have all the answers inside of you to guide you to your desired outcome. Sometimes I may give a suggestion

to see if that fits, but it is always up to you to decide whether it is a fit for you or not. You won't hurt my feelings if it does not.

While in a conversation we may also frame in the form of a summary statement. This means that we make a 1 sentence statement on what the conversation is about: "It sounds like this is about self esteem." Or we can frame a certain behavior: "When you are doing x, are you making it personal?" By giving it a name, it is easier for our client to grab hold of it and get an understanding of how they create their own experience.

Giving Feedback

At times, in a coaching session, we will need to give our client feedback on what they are saying, their beliefs, actions, etc. The way in which we do this is going to determine in large part whether it is received in the way that it is intended.

Here is a checklist to provide feedback through:

Rapport first!

As with everything in coaching, it is important to establish relationship first. Building rapport is critical in giving feedback.

Request permission

We all know that unsolicited advice sucks. I read somewhere that it actually activates the pain center in the brain. Now, whether or not that is true, I don't know. What I do know, is that it made perfect sense to me.

In coaching, we ask permission to give feedback, to confront, etc., at the beginning of the work we will do together with our client. Usually that already starts when they come in for an introductory session. It is pre-framed, meaning that we let our client know beforehand that they can expect us to give feedback.

Specificity

In order for our client to be able to recognize what we are talking about, the feedback needs to be specific. This means that we give examples of when we noticed them say or do something, and explain what we see or hear. At times it is even helpful to show them, using our gestures and voice, what we saw. In that way we act as a mirror.

Tentative

We also want to let our client (or anyone we give feedback to) know that it is based on what we saw or heard. It is from our perspective. That means that we may have missed something.

Separate person from behavior

We are not what we do. That's the premise from which we want to give feedback. At least, if we want to maximize the chance that our client receives it in such a way that it helps build awareness and creates a willingness to look at it.

Example: "You are very global," rather than "I have noticed that 3 times now you have used global words (such as relaxed, confident, optimistic) when I asked you what you'd feel in your body when you have your desired outcome. Are you aware of that?"

Timeliness

The most effective time to give feedback, is in the moment we notice that something happens. In a study that looked at delayed vs. immediate feedback, researchers found that participant who were given feedback immediate were able to make corrections easier and showed significantly larger improvements in performance than those who received delayed feedback.

Make it actionable

Feedback has more impact when your client comes to an understanding of what to do differently. In the case of a coaching conversation you might make it actionable by helping them come up with a menu list of alternatives or by making it part of the coaching outcome.

The Quantum Leap Skills

It is important to note that you will be using the skills of questioning, listening, state induction, and building client awareness for each of the following skills. Here, you are applying those skills towards a specific goal, whether that's getting the strategy process, detecting and analyzing, or any of the other phases of the Quantum Leap system.

Phase I - The Strategy Process

Asking questions to identify the context and trigger of present and desired state, as well as internal response (VAK, beliefs) and resulting behavior. Feeding back the client's strategy process expressing how the client has created their present state or will do their desired state.

Phase II - Detection And Analysis

Identifying frames

Listening for frames that the client presents as part of the present or desired state, then feeding this back to the client to test whether it is a frame. The belief (frame) can be already in place or it can be something the client needs to believe in order to move to their outcome.

Identifying patterns

Listening for a predictable response to similar triggers, then feeding this back to the client to test whether it is a pattern.

Testing for importance of frame / pattern in desired change (Prioritizing)

Asking testing questions to see if changing any of identified patterns or frames will make the biggest difference in achieving the outcome.

Phase III - The How

Testing what to work on (can you / have you)

Asking testing questions that inquire into the client's ability to affect a certain change (make a plan, change a belief, find a new belief, change reference experience),

Asking testing questions that inquire into the client's history to see whether they've done what they want to do before, perhaps in a different scenario. When the answer is yes, inquire whether it works or didn't work, what worked and what didn't work.

Asking "Is this what we need to be working on?"

Phase IV - Setting The Outcome

Inquire about or detect towards motivation

Asking the "why" question 4+ times to get the highest "why"
Feed back a "toward" motivation when the client shares it, and test whether it is why they want the desired outcome
Feed back the client's answers to the questions to induce the state
Check the level of intensity on the state of "toward" motivation

Inquire about or detect away motivation

Asking about the quality of the present state and the cost of continuing to do it that way 4+ times to get the highest "why not"

Feed back an "away from" motivation when you hear it, and test whether it is why they don't want the present state any longer

Feed back the client's answers to induce the state

Check the level of intensity of the state of "away from"

Inquire about pros and cons

Ask about the pros and cons of making the change

Ask about the pros and cons of not making the change

Test what clients says for limiting beliefs / Ask "Is this a limiting belief?"

Ask client to prioritize pros and cons in order of importance / weight

Ask for commitment

Ask closed ended questions to determine client's commitment (Are you fully committed to this outcome? Will you do this?

Test with client for definite "yes!" (Are you sure?)

Setting KPI

Repeating desired state strategy process and checking to see if that would be how we test whether the outcome has been achieved.

Phase IV - Getting The Outcome

Brainstorming For New Inner Game

Asking meta-questions to inquire about possible new beliefs / understandings / decisions

Tasking

Asking questions like:

"What is the one thing you will do (in the coming days or week) to make this a reality in your life?"

"How will you implement this in your day to day activities?"

"What do you need to do to solidify these new frames or learnings?"

Giving a menu list of tasks for client to choose from

Testing

Ask client to try on a new belief, access a resource, etc.

Ask to what extent they are able to access or apply the belief / resource / etc.

Inquire about objections

Inquire into the difference this makes to the outcome

Celebrating

Ask client what works really well

Make gesture or statement to express celebration (i.e. High five)

Holding accountable

Give feedback on what the client said they were going to do, and what they did instead

Hold silence

Ask awareness question to help client step back and reflect.

Part V Focus Points

* There are five types of questions to ask: exploration, clarity, meta-questions, testing and checking questions.
* Exploration questions give you a better understanding on the full story. Clarity questions help ground a conversation. Meta-Questions help you identify current and new beliefs. They also help with activating the necessary energies to create the perseverance and commitment to change (motivation and decision). Testing questions help you identify what you need to work on, what is true for your client and what is not true for your client. And checking questions help you stay on the same page as you check your own understanding of what you've heard your client say.
* As you go through the first four phases of the Quantum

Leap, you will go through the Well-Formed Outcome questions that have been identified in Neuro-Linguistic Programming.

* Listening in coaching is done with the eyes, the ears and the body.

* Inducing states brings meanings and actions together. Coaching is not just about inducing the state, it's about inducing the state in relation to a specific trigger. This is done through going through the QL phases and then making sure that the new states are induced in the body.

* Building awareness (so your client can make informed decisions) is done through setting frames, giving feedback, feeding back the client's stories in the form of the strategy process, confronting and challenging.

{ Part VI }

Supporting Models And Patterns

I n order to gather accurate information from our client, and analyze the gap that exists between present and desired state, there is a need for understanding how we use language. The Meta-Model and Meta-Programs in NLP, as well as the cognitive distortions proposed by Aaron T. Beck's cognitive distortions, work well together and provide you with the necessary tools to unearth a person's reality (whether present or desired) and identify where the limitations are in their current map.

When we communicate with others, we use words to convey what we are experiencing inside and how we see the world. In doing so our "deep structure" information (Noam Chomsky) is lost through deletion, distortion, and generalization. What this means in coaching is that we get the surface level of information, without the specifics of what our client sees, hears and feels when they are sharing their story. This could be because the client isn't aware of the deeper levels themselves, or because they are unable to explain it well.

Richard Bandler and John Grinder, in their book "The Structure of Magic" describe deletions, distortions and generalizations as follows:

Generalization is the process by which elements or pieces of a person's model become detached from their original experience and come to represent the entire category of which the experience is an example. Our ability to generalize is essential to coping with the world. For example, it is useful for us to be able to generalize from the experience of being burned when we touch a hot stove to a rule that hot stoves are not to be touched. But to generalize this experience to a perception that stoves are dangerous and, therefore, to refuse to be in the same room with one is to limit unnecessarily our movement in the world. The same process of generalization may lead a human being to establish a rule such as "Don't express feelings." This rule in the context of a prisoner-of-war camp may have a high survival value and will allow the person to avoid placing himself in a position of being punished. However, that person, using this same rule in a marriage, limits his potential for intimacy by excluding expressions which are useful in that relationship. This may lead him to have feelings of loneliness and disconnectedness — here the person feels that he has no choice, since the possibility of expressing feelings is not available within his model.

Deletion is a process by which we selectively pay attention to certain dimensions of our experience and exclude others. Take, for example, the ability that people have to filter out or exclude all other sound in a room full of people talking in order to listen to one particular person's voice... Deletion reduces the world to proportions which we feel capable of handling. The reduction may be useful in some contexts and yet be the source of pain in others.

Distortion is the process which allows us to make shifts in our experience of sensory data. Fantasy, for example, allows us to prepare for experiences which we may have before they occur. People will distort present reality when rehearsing a speech which they will later present. It is this process which has made possible all the artistic creations which we as humans have produced. A sky as represented in a painting by Van Gogh is possible only as Van Gogh was able to distort his perception of the time-place in which he was located at the moment of creation. Similarly, all the great novels, all the revolutionary discoveries of the sciences involve the ability to distort and misrepresent present reality. Using the same technique, people can limit the richness of their experience.

In short, deleting, distorting and generalizing can lead to limiting states as well as limit the access we have to resources. In coaching, we want to get to the deeper structure of our client's experience. This means helping them work their way back from notions, understandings, conclusions, to their sensory awareness (their primary state). The meta-model provides us with a list of distinctions in which we filter our information and the questions we can ask to **recover the missing details** (see, hear, feel, actions) This process is call "grounding the conversation".

At the same time, we want to **uncover** in which way these filters are limiting our client's states. We use meta-programs and cognitive distortions for this. When we delete and distort information, and make generalizations, it can lead to us being cognitively wrong. This means that we operate from exaggerated and irrational thought patterns that drive problematic and toxic states.

When we habitually use the same kinds of deletions and generalizations to give meaning to something, we create thinking styles (aka meta-program preferences). Below is an overview of the Meta-Model, a short-list of useful meta-programs to listen for and a map of cognitive distortions and their cognitive clearings.

The Meta-Model Distinctions

Meta-model distinction	Questions to ask
Deletions	
"They don't listen to me."	Who specifically does not listen to you?
"People push me around."	Who specifically pushes you around?
"She's a better person."	Better than whom? Better at what?
Unspecified ref. index	
"I am uncomfortable"	Uncomfortable in what way? Uncomfortable when?
"They don't listen to me?"	Who specifically does not listen to you?
"He said that she was	Who specifically said that? Whom did he say that you call mean? What did he mean by 'mean'?
Unspecified verbs	
"Surprisingly, my father lied about his drinking."	How did you feel surprised about that? What surprised you about that?
Nominalizations	
"I don't like unclear people"	Unclear about what in and what?

"The unhappy letter surprised me."	What specifically do you mean with unclear? What indicated to you that her starting to cry occurred slowly?
Universal Quantifiers "She never listens to me."	Never? She has never so much as listened to you a little bit? What do you mean with never? Have there been instances where she did listen to you?
Modal Operators "I have to take care of her." "I can't tell him the truth."	You have to or else what? Who says you have to take care of her? What would happen if you didn't? What would happen if you did?
Complex equivalence "She's always yelling at me; she does not like me."	How do you equate her yelling as meaning she does not like you? Can you recall a time when you yelled at someone that you liked?
Presuppositions	How do you suffer? In what

"If my husband knew how much I suffered, he would not do that."	way? About what? How do you know that your husband does not know this? Why do you assume that his intentions would shift if he knew? Does your husband always use your emotional states to determine his responses?
Cause-effect "You make me sad."	How does my behavior cause you to respond with sad feelings? How specifically does this work?

Table 1: Meta-Model Distinctions (Source: The User's Manual For The Brain by Bob G. Bodenhamer and Dr. L. Michael Hall

Cognitive Distortions

We use language to make sense of the world around us. We label, evaluate, generalize, and delete information in order to understand the world. We do this from a very early age, and a great deal of our mapping the external world around us is set at the age of 5. By that time, our language is limited, and therefore our meaning-making often has distortions in them.

Growing up, we have the ability to make the necessary nuances that will allow us to deal with situations effectively. But that does not always happen. And these cognitive distortions can really hold us back in life. In fact, they can be very toxic.

Below you will find a list of these cognitive distortions, with their cognitive clearings on the right-hand side.

All-or-nothing thinking

You see things in black-or-white categories. If a situation falls short of perfect, you see it as a total failure. When a young woman on a diet at a spoonful of ice cream, she told herself "I've blown my diet completely." This thought upset her so much the she gobbled down an entire quart of ice cream!

Over-generalizing

You see a single negative event, such as a romantic rejection or career reversal, as a never-ending pattern of defeat by using words such a "always" or "never" when you think about it. A depressed salesman became terribly upset when he noticed bird dung on the window shield of his car. He told himself, "Just my luck. Birds are always crapping on my car!"

Mental filter

You pick out a single negative detail and dwell on it exclusively so that your vision of all of reality becomes darkened, like the drop of ink that discolors a beaker of water. Example: You receive many positive comments about your presentation to a group of associates at work, but one of them says something wildly critical. You obsess about his reaction for days and ignore all the positive feedback.

Jumping to conclusions

You interpret things negatively when there are no facts to support your conclusion. Mind reading: Without checking it out, you arbitrarily conclude that someone reacting negatively to you.

Emotional reasoning

You assume that your negative emotions necessarily reflect the way things really are: "I feel terrified about going on airplanes. It must be very dangerous to fly." Or "I feel guilty. I must be a rotten person." Or "I feel angry. This proves I am being treated unfairly." Or "I feel so inferior. This means I am a second-rate person."

"Should" statements

You tell yourself that things *should* be the way you hoped or expected them to be. After playing a difficult piece on a piano, a gifted pianist told herself: "I shouldn't have made so many mistakes." This made her feel so disgusted that she quit practicing for several days. "Musts", "ought's", and "have to's" are similar offenders.

"Should" statements that are directed against yourself lead to guilt and frustration. Should statements directed at others or at the world lead to anger and frustration: "He shouldn't be so stubborn and argumentative." Many people try to motivate themselves with shoulds and shouldn'ts, as if they were delinquents who had to be punished before they could be expected to do anything. "I shouldn't eat that doughnut." This usually does not work because all these shoulds and musts make you feel rebellious and you get the urge to do the opposite. Dr. Albert Ellis calls this "musterbation"

Labeling

Labeling is an extreme form of all or nothing thinking. Instead of thinking "I made a mistake", you attach a negative label to yourself: "I am a loser." Labeling is quite irrational because you are not the same as what you do. Human being exists, but "fools", "losers", and "jerks" do not. These labels are just useless abstractions that lead to anger, anxiety, frustration, and low self esteem.

You may also label others. When someone does something that rubs you the wrong way, you may tell yourself: "He's an

S.O.B." Then you feel that the problem is with the person's character or essence instead of with their thinking or behavior. You see them as totally bad. This makes you feel hostile and hopeless about improving things and leaves little room for constructive communication.

Personalization and blame

Personalization occurs when you hold yourself personally responsible for an event that is not entirely under your control. When a woman received a note that her child was having difficulties at school, she told herself: "This shows what a bad mother I am," instead of trying to pinpoint the cause of the problem so she could be helpful to her child. When another woman's husband beat her, she told herself: "If only I were better in bed, he wouldn't beat me."

Personalization leads to guilt, shame and over-responsibility.

Some people do the opposite. They blame other people or their circumstances for their problems, and they overlook ways that they might be contributing to the problem: "The reason my marriage is so lousy is because my spouse is totally unreasonable." Blame usually does not work very well because other people will resent being scapegoated and they will toss the blame right back. It also creates powerlessness by not taking responsibility.

Catastrophizing

This is a particularly extreme and painful form of fortune telling, where we project a situation into a disaster or the worst-case scenario. You might think catastrophizing helps you prepare and protect yourself, but it usually causes needless anxiety and worry. A person who is catastrophizing might fail an exam and immediately think he or she has likely failed the entire course. A person may not have even taken the exam yet and already believe he or she will fail—assuming the worst, or preemptively catastrophizing.

Fortune telling

We believe we know what the future holds, as if we have psychic powers. We make negative predictions, feeling convinced these are unavoidable facts. Examples of fortune telling: "I am going to fail," "This situation will never change."

Impossibility thinking

Imposing semantic limits on oneself and others using the word "can't" which presupposes that there is some law or rule that constrains us from doing something.

Discounting

This extreme form of all-or-nothing thinking occurs when a person discounts positive information about a performance, event, or experience and sees only negative aspects. A person engaging in this type of distortion might disregard any compliments or positive reinforcement he or she receives.

Table 2: Cognitive Distortions

Cognitive distortion	Problem it creates	Cognitive clearing
All-or-nothing thinking	Eliminates and hides all values in between the polar choices. Sets up extremes as in manic-depression Undermines creativity and choices. Creates obsessions, compulsions.	Both-and / In-between thinking. Test situation to see if there is some option in-between the extremes. To what degree? Gauge for percentages, scale from 0 to 10. Check contexts. Outcome: expands choice
Over-generalizing	Limits finer distinctions, and blinds to possibilities for solutions	Contextual thinking. Inquire about the context of the information by asking: what, where, which, who, why. Ask about specifics. Outcome: clarity and precision
Mental filter	Limits full perspective. Blinds one from seeing beyond the tunnel vision.	Perspective thinking . Step back and identify filters that create tunnel vision. Take third-person perspective to empathize with anoth-

		er's view Outcome: expands awareness to see other perspectives.
Jumping to conclusions	Limits seeing and dealing with a person based on facts of sensory data. Projects beliefs onto others.	Current sensory information What are the facts? See-hear-feel facts? Ask: How do you know that? How draw that conclusion? What are the probabilities? What are you feeling or thinking? Outcome: straightens out relationship, encourages dialogue, keep things present.
Emotional Reasoning	Limits choice by creating an emotional determinism. Impairs healthy use of emotions.	Witness-thinking . Step back and just observe. Witness senses, facts, activities without making any judgment. Suspend evaluation; witness what is. Outcome: increases choices and options, stops the coloring of things by emotions, obtain cleaner information.

Should state-ments	Limits a sense of choice. Leashes one to a sense of dreadful duty. Eliminates sense of choice.	Choice thinking . Test "should," "must," and "have to." Why? Who says? What is the rule? What is the demand? Change to "want" or "prefer." Outcome: prevents addiction and build up of pressure. Keeps wants and de-sires healthy.
Labeling	Sells a person short by putting into a box and assuming that's all the person is. Hides reality in a label.	Reality testing. Ask: Is this just a label, just a word? Explore: In what way is it bad, undesira-ble? What are you re-ferring to? When? Where? Under what conditions? Outcome: more accurate map-ping.
Personalization and blame	Blaming limits recognizing re-sponse-ability. Wastes energy accusing some-one. Blinds one to responses for change.	Ask: what am I re-sponse-able for? To whom? Is this a re-sponse that others make? Question the nominalization – What is the process? The ac-tion?

	Impairs power of responsibility.	What action has been "named" (nominalized)? What is the system? Who is in it? How does the system work? Outcome: Clarity, see processes rather than things.
Catastrophizing	Limits problem-solving skills. Prevents one from working on creative solutions. Misdirects energy to whining and complaining.	Meta-cognitive thinking. Ask about patterns and structures above and beyond the story and content. Identify thinking patterns. Question words and terms for what they refer to. Outcome: Expand awareness of factors in the back of the mind, see and identify patterns and leverage points of change.
Fortune telling	Limits hope, belief, vision, dreaming, possibilities. Makes problems permanent and so eliminates solutions.	Tentative predictive thinking . Study trends, factors, and causes that contribute to an experience. Study consequences and probabilities. Outcome:

		Opens future, identifies leverage points, increase ability to influence.
Impossibility thinking	Limits ideas about what's possible. Stunts ideas of human potential Impairs ability to dream and to take risks.	Possibility thinking . Test "can'ts." Is physical or psychological "can't?" Ask: What stops you? "Do you have permission? "What would it look, sound or feel like?"

Meta-Programs

Another way of detecting patterns in what your client is sharing, is through listen to their thinking style. This is the lens we use to interpret what happens around us.

The following thinking styles describe *the kinds of lenses* we use when we look at people, events, and information. Use the following to profile your preferences and tendencies. Identify where you operate from with a check and then indicate the range of flexibility with brackets. *(Source: Figuring Out People by Dr. L. Michael Hall)*

Internal Referencing ——————— *External Referencing*

People with internal as a preference know from within whether they did something well or not so good. They rely on their own inner frame of reference. They collect information and use their intuition to decide. Typical expressions are "I had that feeling" or "I simply knew it." They have autonomy in their decisions. They know by themselves what is right. It is difficult to persuade these people in case of a different opinion. They react less to praise or criticism. Both will rather be used to judge whether the other understands the subject or not. For them it is helpful to learn to listen to proposals and feedback from others.

People with this preference are open minded in their decisions. They want to know what others think. "Someone has to tell me" or "I was appreciated". They have to get the information for evaluation from the outside. They want to know what others think of them. They react to positive comments or critique. Persons with strong external references need information from outside sources to know where they stand. Thus they are less autonomous. For them, it is helpful to learn not to get too influenced by others and to rely on people whom you know very well and whom you can trust.

Reactive ———————————————————— *Active*

If a report would need to be written with a four-week deadline, a person with the Active thinking preference would start to prepare the report after maybe two weeks' time. Changes are dealt with at once and spontaneously. This thinking preference is important for short reaction times. A person with the reactive thinking preference would begin to write during the last two or three days. Changes are dealt with only after thorough reflection. This preference is useful in quality control jobs.

Long term ———————————————————— *Short term*

People with the long term preference put their emphasis on midterm or long- term consequences and effects. They tend to overlook short-term consequences. They prefer to use a time planner. They divide time globally. Long-term means to you in the current job situation: The prime attention for short term is focused on the immediate or short-term consequences. They tend to ignore the long-term aspects. They have a more "southern" feeling of time. Their feeling for time is more like that of southern cultures and therefore they use time planners much less. This thinking preference is important for immediate reactions and for improvisation.

Global ——————————————————— *Detail*

People with the global preference generalize. They like to have an overview first. The chunks they are using carry rough and more global information. They concentrate on the general direction of a project. They can easily see relations and basic structures. They work best when they can delegate details to others. Their learning style is from the Global to Details (deductive).

People using the details preference concentrate on the details of a job. Details are important to them. The chunks they are using carry many detailed bits of information and have a finer structure. They deal with the elements and components of a project. Preciseness and accuracy is important to them. Their learning style is from Details to Global (inductive).

Options ——————————————————— *Procedures*

People with the options preference are motivated to find new solutions and to experiment with alternatives whenever they get a chance to do so. They ask: "How else could it work?". If you give them a process that promises 100 percent success, they tend to polish it even further. To them decisions mean limitations. They do not like decisions and if they happen to be Re-Active at the same time, they avoid decisions. They avoid or ignore rules and look for alternatives to the routine path. People in this preference can be motivated by giving them options, opportunities, alternatives and chances. They can easily develop procedures, but have difficulty in following them.

In the procedures preference people are looking for the right way and for proven procedures. They ask: "What do I have to do?". Their frame of reference is to do what is necessary. They like to go the official way and follow firm working structures. They have no problem deciding, any decision is a relief to them. Once they have found a procedure that works, they will always return to it.

They will be irritated or confused if someone asks them to break rules. "Why should I break rules which obviously worked?". Giving them proven procedures and processes can best motivate these people. If you do not provide them with procedures, they can become helpless. They have difficulty in developing procedures. They like to be given procedures and like to follow them.

Caring for Self
Caring for Others

To people with the caring for self preference it is more important to first concentrate on oneself. Probably they would realize that they need something to drink before they see that the others need something too before they go and get the drinks. This thinking preference is often used by athletes or in professions in which performance is very important.

People with the caring for others preference take care of others first. In our example, they would notice that someone else needs something to drink and would go and get it. In this situation, they would likely get something to drink for them self too. This thinking preference is often found in service and support jobs and in healing professions.

Difference ——————————————————— *Sameness*

People with a sameness preference look first in any new situation for whether this has something in common with previous experiences. They sometimes have difficulty in noticing differences and changes and they dislike major changes. They like the familiar things and the safety of the known. This preference is important to recognize patterns.

People with the difference thinking preference first recognize any differences based on their past experience. When they enter a new room or meet a new situation, they can immediately detect what is different compared with what they know from the past. They have difficulties in recognizing patterns or similarities, and they like change. This thinking preference is important for spotting mistakes.

Relationship ——————————————————— *Task*

People who primarily concentrate on the persons involved are mainly concerned with the well-being of these persons. In case of a strong tendency towards this preference the task gets out of focus. They put their attention on people and on the team spirit. They tend to care for other people. People with task orientation are mainly interested in getting the job done and reaching the goal. In the extreme, this can result in pushing colleagues or themselves too hard. They put their attention on the work or job to be done and to the related dates and deadlines. They are attracted by tasks.

Towards ——————————————————— **Away From**

People in this preference move towards a certain goal. They quickly leave the past behind and quickly address their tasks and goals. In extreme situations it can mean they want to get to the goal and overlook the problems on the way. Their motivation is the attractiveness of their goals. For them it is often helpful to find out what kind of problems may arise by achieving their goal.

Problem oriented people move away from all sorts of problems. They follow an avoidance-strategy, they like to avoid problems or difficulties, their attention is directed towards things that shall not happen. They can use this preference, their caution, positively to deliver high quality, to proceed in a safe manner and thus become very reliable. They match very well with their "Towards" colleagues. They can best be motivated by being shown negative consequences. For them it is often helpful to find out what exactly they want to have instead of having the problem they are solving.

In Time ——————————————————— **Through Time**

People who are in-time oriented will be great at being present, yet struggle to predict how long a task or action will take. They are often late with deadlines, meetings, or events.

Through time people often see their timeline right in front of them, whereas someone with a preference for in-time often has their timeline run through them with their future in front and past behind them. This means that through-time people can see time and plan and monitor progress. They are better at being punctual and meeting deadlines.

Patterns and Processes

In Phase II where we detect and analyze the patterns in the present state and missing elements in the desired state, there is a list of elements that make part of the system of an experience. As we go through a process of prioritization, we discover which element will make the biggest difference in the change work we do in coaching.

NLP and Neuro-Semantics patterns focus on changing these elements, so in this part of the book each you will find a pattern or two for each of the elements to change.

Meta-Stating

The actual process of meta-stating is actually very simple—*accessing* a thought or emotion and *apply* it to another state (i.e., thought, emotion, or physiology). That's the short and quick approach. *Access and apply.*

With *accessing* is *amplifying* to get enough of the state. And within *applying* is *appropriating to life contexts and analyzing* to quality control the end result and effects. This give us a total of 5 **steps** —all when start with **A.** This **5** words that start with **A** make the basic meta-stating process easier to remember. Colin Cox has suggested two more words that begin with A. One of them is prior (*awareness*) and one of them is after (*accelerate*).

** Awareness

Become aware of your state and what resource you want to apply to it.

1. **Access a resource state.**

What resource state do you want to bring to bear on or apply to the primary state? A "resource" can be a thought, feeling, idea, belief, value, memory, imagination.

2. **Amplify fully and anchor.**

Juice up the resource state and establish an anchor for it by touch, sight, sound, word, etc.   Do you have a sufficiently strong enough state with which to work?

3. **Apply** *to the primary state. Bring* the resource *to bear* on the primary state (this creates meta-level anchoring), or embed the primary state inside a resource state.

4. **Appropriate** *to your life, to specific contexts, or to the future (future pacing).*

Where do you want to experience this meta-state? Imagine having this layered consciousness in your mind as your frame as you move out into your future.

5. **Analyze the quality, health, balance (ecology) of the system.**

Would it enhance your life to set this resource as your frame-of-reference for the primary state experience? Would every facet of your mind-and-body align with this?

Detection and Analysis #1 – Limiting Belief

Meta-Stating confirmation / disconfirmation for belief change

Elicitation Questions:

What limiting belief stands in the way of your genius state? Do you have any belief that undermines your self-actualization and prevents you from living fully?

The Pattern:

1. **Identify the limiting and empowering beliefs.**

Ecology for this pattern occurs before you begin. So make sure you have a *high quality idea* that you want to confirm and transform into a belief. What enhancing and empowering beliefs would you really like to have running in your mind-and-emotions? What limiting belief stands in the way of your genius state? How does this belief sabotage you or undermine your effectiveness? Have you had enough? What empowering belief would you like to have in its place? Is the new idea realistic? Is it useful, productive, enhancing in all aspects of your life?

2. **Access a strong and robust state of "No!"**

Think of something that every fiber in your body can say "No!" to in a way that is fully congruent. *Menu:* Would you push a little child in front of a speeding bus just for the hell of it? Would you eat a bowl of dirty filthy worms when you have delicious food available? Say that *"No!"* again and again while you take a moment to notice it, make an internal snapshot of it so that you know how it feels, how you breathe, look, sound, hold your posture, etc. *Anchor* your *"No!"* with your hand gestures. Feel it. Hear your voice of "No!"

3. Apply your "No!" to the limiting belief.

Ask a series of questions: Do you want this (limiting) belief? Does it serve you? Enhance your life? Empower you as a person? Evoke a strong feeling of a powerful *"No"* as you think about wanting to keep the belief that you know is stupid, useless, limiting belief. And you can keep on saying *No!* to the value of the limiting belief until you begin to feel that you have dis-confirmed it and it no longer has any power over you, that it has no more room in your presence, in your mind. How many more times and with what voice, tone, gesturing, do you need to totally disconfirm the old belief so that you know —deep inside yourself—that it will no longer run your programs?

4. Access a strong and robust "Yes!"

Think about something that every fiber of your being says *"Yes!"* to without any question or doubt. Do you have anything like that? Notice your "Yes!" Notice the neurology and feeling of your "Yes!" Notice the voice of "Yes!" How do you best gesture the "Yes!" with your hands and body so that it amplifies your feelings? How much have you amplified your "Yes!"?

5. Meta "Yes!" the enhancing belief.

As you feel this *"Yes!"* let's make it a strong emotional *yes* and now repeatedly say it to the   empowering belief that you want to send a command to your nervous system. Do you want   this? [*"Yes!"*] Really? How many more times do you need to say *"Yes!"* right now in order to   feel that you have fully welcomed it into your presence?

6. Validate the "Yes!" with higher-level Yeses.

This is only an exercise and so you can't keep this! You really want this? Will this improve your life? Will it be valuable to you? Will it make a difference in your life?   Will it enable you to unleash new potentials? Oh, you want this?

Releasing Judgment

Distinctions: The judgments that you have spent a lifetime developing are valuable and useful in most contexts of life. It is not useful in the coaching context. The mind-set and attitude of automatically *judging yourself or others* works against you in coaching. It undermines your progress and interferes with hearing the client on the client's terms. Both *self-judgment* and *judgment of others* are dragon states to be tamed and/or slain.

Elicitation Questions:

When and where does judgment arise when you are coaching? When and where does your judgments interfere with your ability to listen and support?

The Pattern:
1. Identify your experience of judgment.

When and where does judgment arise in you? Identify specific time when you experienced judgment: When and where does it interfere with your ability to listen and support someone? How do you know it is judgment? How do you know it interferes? How do you represent that? Voice, picture, words? What is the state you experience?

2. Quality control the judgment experience.

Is this state enhancing, enriching, empowering of you or the other person? Does this state enable you to listen and support in a caring and compassionate way? Will judgment help your coaching? Do you need it then? Are you ready to release it and replace it with better resources?

3. Access the replacement states.

A) Pure or mere observation.

When have you just observed something without judgment? Have you ever been in an audience and watched a movie, a play, a concert? Have you ever sat in a balcony and just watched? Have you ever gone to a mall where there were layers and levels of floors and looked down? What is it like in your body when you are just observing?

B) Acceptance

What best enables you to access a state of acceptance? What is that like for you? How does it feel?

C) Appreciation

What triggers you to melt in appreciation? What is that like?

Transition: Access and use a state of releasing for transitioning from judging to just listening and supporting.

How do you release and let go of something? Menu list: muscle tension > relax; breathing; saying goodbye; closing a door; relieving yourself, balloons floating off,   opening a window, etc. Apply releasing to judgment when you are coaching. What happens? How is that? Is the judgment released?

Now having released the judgment, bring in the 3 resourceful states to replace the judgment.

4. Check for objections.

Are there any objections to doing this? If yes, what is the objection? What is the meaning, the belief, etc. to be reframed? Retest until there are no objections and the releasing of judgment settles well within. Test to   see if in the place of judgment there is now witnessing, acceptance, and appreciation.

5. Future pace.

Imagine the coaching session you will do tomorrow ... As you put this in your future in the coming days, what is that like for you?

Detection and Analysis #2 – Cognitive Distortion

Meta-Stating Cognitive Distortions

1. Identify the "dragon" cognitive style/s.

How do you think about that event, its meanings, its significance, what it means about you and your life? When you go through the checklist of the cognitive distortions, which ones stand out regarding your meanings? What are the three biggest cognitive distortions that you have found so far?

2. Identify the cognitive correction for the style of thinking and reasoning.

"It sounds like you are thinking about this using Personalizing. As you step back from it, does it seem accurate?" If so or if not, how else would you characterize your pattern of thinking   and reasoning? How long have you used this cognitive distortion in making meaning of things? Has it served you well? In what way? In what way may it have undermined your sense of well-being and accurate processing? What is the cognitive correction that provides a more enhancing and accurate reasoning style? What more useful way of processing this information would you like to use? Are you willing to try it on and give it a chance?

3. **Meta-state the cognitive distortion to reduce its influence.**

What would you best like to do to reduce its power? Would you like to challenge, dispute, and argue against Personalizing, Over-generalizing, Should-ing, etc.? Are you ready to identify and release these cognitive patterns? What else will bring these patterns into the light where you can deal with them? What else will break their power of working outside of consciousness?

4. **Meta-state to cognitive correction to create an attractor frame**

What do you need to feel or understand about the cognitive correction for it to become part of your way of thinking? What state could you texture it with, that would help you reach your outcome?

5. **Future pace and confirm.**

As you imagine moving forward with this today, tomorrow, this week ... how does this fit? Are you fully aligned with this? Are there any objections to this?

Meta-Stating Ownership

This pattern enables us to recognize and own our core "powers" or functions. By meta- stating our core powers, and owning them, we can create the foundation for *personal empowerment* and then the more complex states of responsibility, proactivity, initiative, and risk-taking.

The Pattern:

> 1. **Access a full experience of your Four Central Powers.**

Notice that you have two private inner powers. You have powers of:

Thinking: representing,   believing, valuing, understanding, reasoning, etc.
Emoting: feeling, somatizing, valuing, etc.

You also have two public or outer powers by which you can effect yourself and the world:

Speaking: languaging, using and manipulating symbols, asserting, etc.
Behaving: acting, responding, relating, etc.

Just notice and enjoy and appreciate these as you access them fully. Access them so that you begin to feel these powers. Use your hands to mime out these *powers* in your own personal "space" to create your *Circle of Power* and influence and responsibility.

2.   Access and Amplify the Resource State of Ownership.

Think about something that you can say "Mine!" to fully, that every fiber in your body knows that it is yours. Has there ever been a time when you said **"Mine!'** that fully? Recall that time. Be there. Feel it when you strongly sense that something is yours, when every fiber in your being says, ***"Mine!"*** Keep it small and simple: "My hand!" "My eye." "My cat." "My toothbrush."

Find a "Mine!" that clearly yours in a positive way, a "Mine!"

3.   Amplify your Ownership states until your Neurology radiates.

Amplify your sense of ownership and say, "This is my *zone* of power. I am totally responsible   for my *responses* of mind, emotion, speech and behavior..." Notice how that transforms things.

4.   Access the States of Acceptance and Appreciation of "Mine!"

Use a small and simple reference to get the feel of acceptance... when you just welcomed and acknowledged   something   ...   a rainy day, the traffic. Now feel this acceptance about what you own as yours. Do the same with a reference for appreciation.

Feel that appreciation about this sense of ownership. Feel that sense of acceptance and appreciation and apply.

5.   Future Pace to install

Imagine in the weeks and months to come, moving through the world with this frame of mind about your zone of response... power... Do you like that? Just notice how it will transform things as it allows you to fully claim you mind, heart, voice, and response powers.

Setting Responsibility To/For Frames

As a Coach, you are *responsible **for*** yourself— what you say and do, the structures and frames that you set up. You are responsible **for** how you interact, treat your participants, the spirit and atmosphere that you set, etc. You are *not* responsible **for** how they think, feel, talk, or act. They are responsible **for** that. Yet you are responsible **to** them... to them as participants, as learners, as colleagues, as human beings. Separating out and stepping into a state of clarity about this Responsibility To/For Distinction therefore empowers you in relating in a healthy way, not creating sick and dependent relationships, or getting off on the "power" or "authority" that comes along with being out in front as a leader.

The Pattern:

1. **Access your Power Zone**

    Access, acknowledge, and appreciate your four neuro-linguistic powers of thinking-emoting,   speaking and behaving. Step into your power zone and own it fully (bring "ownership" —   as expressed in "mine!" to the Power Zone).

2. **Distinguish between For and To.**

    I am able to respond (response-able) FOR my thinking,

emoting, speaking and behaving. I   own and acknowledge my ability to make such responses. They are mine and I will not hold   anyone else responsible for these powers. I am **not** able to respond (response-able) FOR the thinking, emoting, speaking, or behaving of anyone else! I cannot and will not assume any ownership over their Power Zone. It belongs to them. I acknowledge that, appreciate that, and will honor that.

3. **Step into this Experience fully and feel it as you Gesture it.**

Feel it in your muscles. Let it become part of your muscle memory. Invent awesome and   memorable phrases for expressing *the to-for principle.*

"If it does not come out of my mind, my mouth, my heart, my body... it's not mine!" "I will not insult others by treating them as fragile, weak, and unable to claim their personality powers."

"I have my own full time job being responsible for myself." "I refuse to act in a co-dependent way thinking I need to rescue others." "I will only invite others to contract with me for assistance, I refuse to be seduced into fixing them or cramming it down their throats."

"I don't have to or need to rescue anyone. Others have the right to choose to be as un-sane as they want to be! Especially family members!" I will respect others to be responsible *for* themselves. I love others enough to believe in them and their response-abilities. I will trust that others can assume responsibility for themselves."

4. Apply to Coaching.

Imagine a training group or an individual person who has contracted for you to coach. Apply the Responsibility To/For Distinction to that relationship. Giving permission, protecting, avoiding any feel of "manipulation" or playing with them in a negative way.

Meta-Stating Self

1. **Access the three "A" resource states of Acceptance, Appreciation, and Awe.**

Access each states by using a small and simple referent so that you can access the feeling of the state fully.

Acceptance:

Have you ever accepted something? Think of something small and simple that you can easily accept without particularly liking or wanting, but you put with it.

Appreciation:

Is there anything that you really appreciate? That you melt in appreciation?

Awe:

What is so big, so wonderful, so marvelous, so incredible that you stand in awe of it, speechless, in utter wonder?

2. **Amplify each state and apply to self.**

Amplify each state until you have a robust enough state. Set up a sliding anchor on the arm of this continuum of welcoming responses. Apply acceptance to the things about yourself that you know you should accept but you find challenging to accept, your shadow side, experiences that have happened to you, the cards that life dealt you. Accept your overall sense of self and life.

Apply appreciation to your sense of self as doer and achiever. Appreciate your over-all self,   and every gift, talent, and strength.

Apply awe and esteem to your self as a valuable, precious, magnificent human being unconditionally.

3. **Separating self-confidence and self-esteem, use self-esteem to enrich self-appreciation and self-acceptance.**

Feeling this self-esteem fully and completely, letting it grow and expand . . . that's right,   now notice what else you can appreciate (fire anchor) and what else you can just accept (fire   anchor) more gracefully and easily.

4. **Apply self-esteeming, appreciating, and accepting in needed contexts**

Is there any context, situation, or event wherein you feel tempted to self-contempt, self-question, self-doubt, and/or self-dislike yourself? In what context would you prefer a more resourceful response? As you think about that, I want you to feel this esteem (fire anchor)   for yourself knowing that your worth and value is a given and feel this appreciation for what you can do so that you focus there, and feel this acceptance of the things that just are that you have to deal with.

5. **Apply self-esteeming to the old self-contempting context**

Now especially notice how feeling this esteem and self-awe at the mystery of you and your potentials it transforms this old context, doesn't it? Do you like that? Would that make a difference? Are you ready to self-respect yourself no matter what?

6. **Imaginatively put into your future to validate.**

Imagine moving through life in the weeks and months to come with this frame of mind. Do you like this? Notice how this would transform things for you . . . Does every aspect of the higher parts of your mind fully agree with this? Are you un-stoppable?

7. **Dis-Identify yourself from your Powers, Roles, Experiences, History, etc.**

Access your power zone and dis-identify from each power, one at a time.

"I think yet I am more than my thoughts."

"I emote yet I am more than my emotions."

"I speak yet I am more than my words and speech."

"I act yet I am more than my behaviors."

Access your sense of self and step back to dis-identify yourself from being narrowly defined by your experiences, roles, definitions, etc.

"I experience all kinds of things every day, yet I am more than any experience."

"I perform various roles, yet I am more than my roles."

"I have gone through many things yet I am more than my history."

8.   Identify yourself as an Emergent "Much More ... "

"I stubbornly refuse to narrowly define myself and box myself into narrow definitions based on money, looks, degrees, experiences ... so that I can stubbornly stand for becoming and developing and discovering all that I can become."

Self Esteeming: The Gamechanger Protocol

Before we get down to it I just want to reiterate that getting feedback from your body is a slow process requiring patience. Once you ask a specific 'What's that about?' question, you need to wait ... and as you keep that question in mind ... wait some more.

For first time Scanners (you will learn more about this as you go through the steps of the process) it can take up to a minute or more of sitting with a question to get feedback. And that's okay.

Scanning step by step:

1. **Get a pen and a blank piece of paper.**

Draw a line in the middle of the page and split it into two columns: A and B. Once you are sitting down comfortably, feeling relaxed and with all possible disturbances removed write down in Column A at the bottom of the page: 'I am okay.' You should start at the bottom of the page and work your way up. (The belief 'I am okay' is the first healthy belief you are going to Scan in.)

2. **The next step is to write down the answer to the 'I am okay' set-up question**

'What would it mean to me if I could know and experience that I am okay fully and completely no matter what?' If your answer is positively stated write it down, one line up, in Column A. If your answer is about what you don't want, for example, 'I won't be scared anymore' write it down in Column B (one line up) and ask yourself the question: 'So if I am not that what would I be instead?' Write that answer in Column A on the same line.

3. **Now think about your last answer in Column A**

and ask yourself: 'Having that, what would that mean to me?' and write the answer down one line up. If it's positively stated it falls into Column A and negatively falls into Column B.

4. **Keep on answering the 'Having that what would that mean to me?' question**

five times or more whilst focusing on the last answer in Column A. You must still use the same writing process (Column A for positively stated and Column B for negatively stated). The process of building up this positive energy is called Supercharging. Stop doing this step only when you start to feel yourself smile or your face feels full of positive energy.

5. **Focus on taking all the positive energy from the words written down in Column A**

Imagine all that energy concentrated in your hand. Start "scanning" the energy into every cell of your body by moving your hand from the top of your head down to your feet. Do it slowly from your head down to your feet and back again as if you were using a handheld CAT scanner – your hand being the scanner. (It's important to actually use your hand.)

6. Form an open palm gesture with your hand –

(an open hand shape with the palm facing inwards, towards yourself and your elbow up in line with your ears). Now tell every cell in your body: 'I give myself full permission to have this' where this is all the positive Supercharged meanings and energy you have created in Column A. Slowly move your hand (Open Palm Scan) from the top of your head, down to your face, neck, torso, stomach, lower body and legs - all the way down to your feet, so that every cell in every part of your body can now have this. Then move slowly up again. It should take about 20 to 30 seconds to move all the way down and another 20 to 30 seconds for moving all the way up, if you have no Wobbles or 'interruptions.'

7. If you feel a Wobble (block) or 'interruption':

Write down (on a new page) where in the body you are experiencing the Wobble (e.g. neck, chest, stomach etc.) Now focus on the Wobble and ask yourself the question: 'What's this about?' (This process is called translating a Wobble.) This answer will emerge slowly, so focus on the energy of the Wobble and keep the 'What's that about?' question in mind for 60-90 seconds – an answer will begin to form which will probably start out as being vague. Don't judge it, just explore it. Once you have your first answer write it down next to where you wrote what the source of the Wobble is.

8. **Once you have your first answer you may need to ask more 'What's that about?'**

Or other clarity questions: 'Whose voice is that?', 'Who says that it's impossible?', 'How do you know this will never work for you?', 'Doubts about what?'... etc. Keep asking clarifying questions until you can create a specific movie in your mind about what the Wobble is about.

9. **Once the message is clear use The Decision Tree to Keep, Solve or Let go this message.**

If the answer is Keep: thank that part of you for helping you be your best and the energy of the Wobble should disappear. If the answer is Solve: work out the best way to solve this (action, conversation or hidden benefits need to be uncovered). If you have solved it accurately the energy should disappear. If you have partially solved it, the energy will change or move. If that happens write down where the new energy is or the new level of energy (if it hasn't moved) and use the 'What's that about?' question to translate this new Wobble. Write it down and then use The Decision Tree to work with the next layer of what's going on. If you want to let go: Focus on the phrase you want to let go and say to yourself 'I give myself full permission to let go of as much of this as I can for today.' If you have partially let it go, the energy will change or move. If that happens write down where the new energy is or the new level of energy (if it hasn't moved) and use the 'What's that about?' question to translate this new Wobble. Write it down and use The Decision Tree to work with the next layer of what is going on.

10. You will know when you've effectively dealt with a Wobble as the energy will no longer be there.

Once that happens, it's time to reconnect with the built-up energy of the Supercharge by either reading through the words you have written down in Column A from the bottom of the page up, or by answering the meaning questions again. Once you feel the energy on your face again use the Open Palm Scan moving down from the position of your last Wobble. Scan all the way to your feet and back again, (going up and down should take you around 40 seconds if there are no Wobbles).

11. Once you have addressed all your Wobbles:

And have either dealt with them fully or made progress with them (as is the case when you are chipping away at letting something go), it's time to Lock it down. You lock it down by asking yourself, 'What does it mean to me that I am more and more aligned with being okay?' (or whichever new empowering belief that you are focusing on). Then once you have that answer ask yourself 'What does that mean to me?' five times or more. You need to follow the same rules as before, if it is negatively stated write it in Column B and then find the positively stated answer instead, 'So If I don't have that, what will I have instead?' This step-by-step process can be used to Scan in any of the 10 Game Changer Protocol beliefs.

Source: Goodenough, Tim (2016-07-13). Game Changer Protocol: Free yourself from limiting beliefs and supercharge your life

Detection and Analysis #3: Meta-Program Preference

Stretching Meta-Programs

Meta-Programs inform your brain about two things: what to attend to and *what to delete.* If you move toward values, you delete awareness about what you move away from. If you sort for the details, you delete the big picture. To change this or to expand this, re-direct awareness to what you normally delete, value that information, and practice looking for it.

Example:
If you have typically operated using the Other-Referencing meta-program and you give yourself permission to shift to Self-Referencing. Yet when you do, you hear an internal voice that sounds like your mother's voice in tone and tempo, "It's selfish to think about yourself. Don't be so selfish, you will lose all of your friends." This voice objects on two accounts: selfishness and disapproval that leads to loneliness. So rephrase your permission to take these objections into account.

"I give myself permission to see the world referencing centrally from myself—my values, beliefs, wants, etc., knowing that my values including loving, caring, and respecting others and that this will keep me balanced by considering the effect of my choices on others."

The Pattern:

1. **Awareness: Identify and check the ecology of the current meta-program filter.**

When, where, and how do you use this meta-program which does not serve you well? How does it undermine your effectiveness in some way?

2. **Describe the preferred meta-program filter.**

What meta-level processing would you prefer to run your perceiving and valuing? *Contexts*: When, where, and how do you want this meta-program to govern your consciousness? *If having any difficulties, then] Model the new meta-program.* Do you know someone who uses this meta-program? If so, then explore with that person   his or her experience until you can fully step into that position. When you can, then step into 2nd perception so that you can see the world out of that person's meta-program eyes, hearing what he or she hears, self-talking as he or she engages in self-dialogue, and feeling what that person feels. What's that like?

3. **Give yourself permission for expanding the meta-program.**

Do you have permission to expand this meta-program? As you give yourself permission, what are you aware of? How well does it settle? If there are objections or fears that you sense, what are they? Do you have permission to shift to this meta-program filter? What happens when you give yourself permission to use it for a time? Are there any objections? Answer by reframing and then future pace.

4. Experiment with trying out the extended meta-program.

Imaginatively adopt the new meta-program, pretend to use it in sorting, perceiving, attending, etc. Notice how it seems, feels, works, etc. in some contexts where you think it would serve you better. Even if it seems a little "weird" and strange due to your unfamiliarity with looking at the world with that particular perceptual filter, notice what other feelings, beside discomfort, may arise with it.

5. Run a systems check on the meta-program filter.

Go meta to an even higher level and consider what this meta-program will do to you and for you in terms of perception, valuing, believing, behaving, etc. What kind of a person would it begin to make you? What effect would it have on various aspects of your life?

6. Set multiple frames for the new extended meta-program.

What ideas or beliefs would support this to filter things? What meaning would make this more significant and valuable for you? What decision or intention?

7. **Future pace using the meta-program in specific contexts.**

Practice, in your imagination, using the meta-program and do so until it begins to feel comfortable and familiar.

Detection and Analysis #4: Toxic Reference Experience

Meta-Stating Events

1. Identify the "dragon" event.

What sabotages you from your highest and best? From your genius flow state? What about that creates the sabotage? The problem? The limitation? What do you use as your reference event or point when you think about that? Has there been an especially hurtful or traumatic event in your life?

2. Meta-state the referent event.

Are you clear that you have been using a poor, inadequate, disastrous, or toxic reference? Are you willing to stop it? To refuse that reference? Are you willing to begin to build and use more positive and life-enhancing references? What references will you use from this day forward? Describe it fully. As you take this on, what are the new beliefs you will create about this?

3. Future pace and confirm.

As you imagine moving forward with this today, tomorrow, this week ... how does this fit? Are you fully aligned with this? Are there any objections to this?

Change Personal History

1. Access a problematic memory

Are there any problematic, unwanted, or unpleasant feelings that you want to deal with? What are they? Do you have a memory that corresponds to this less than resourceful feeling? Elicit it fully and set an anchor for that state.

2. Invite the person into a trans derivational search

As you take this feeling (fire anchor), let it guide you back in time ... back along your time-line, and assist you in remembering other times where you felt this same kind of feeling. Allow yourself to float back, all the way back to previous times and places where you felt this ... Good. As you re-experience that negative state again, just stop and observe your age. How old do you feel yourself to be in this experience? As you continue this historical search for other times and places where you felt this, can you go back through time and find three to six experiences of this same negative state? (Ask about the person's age as you keep re-anchoring the state. When you get back to the earliest one, stop.)

3. Break state to interrupt and to anchor new resources

As you now step out of that younger you, let yourself just objectively observe that memory and do so from your adult self. As you look back on those experiences, what specific resources would you need in those past situations for that younger you to have responded in a more effective way? Do you know these resources? How easily can you access them so that we can anchor these resourceful states?

4. Collapse resourceful anchor with the unresourceful anchor

When you return to the earliest experience, I want you to feel this (simultaneously fire both the negative anchor and the resource anchor). What is that like? How do you experience the past memory now when you know you have this resource with you? How does this resource make that past different? Now, I want you to come up through history, stopping at each past experience with the new resource, so that history begins changing, so that each experience becomes more resourceful and satisfying.

5. Trouble-shooting

If you have difficulty changing the past experience, then let's come up to the present and construct and anchor more powerful resources and stack them on your resource anchor.

6. Break state and test

Once you have changed all of the past experiences, I want you to break state. What did you eat for breakfast? Now let's see what happens when you think about that problematic feeling. What happens? Have the memories changed? In what way? Does the person experience the resource as there?

7. Future pace

What happens for you when you think about similar possible experiences that may occur in the future now that you have these new resources with you?

Detection and Analysis #5: Troubling Relationship With Emotions

Drop Down Through

1. **Identify the experience and emotion you want to transform.**

What emotion, feeling, memory, or experience would you like to transform so that it enhances your life? Are there any emotions or experiences that undermine your success that you would like to eliminate?

2. **Step Into that Experience.**

For the purposes of transformation, recall that experience and step into it so that you see what you saw, hear what you heard, and fully   feel what you felt. Be there again. ....Good. Where do you feel this in your body? What does it feel like? How intense are you experiencing this emotion? Good, just be there with it for a moment, noticing ... just noticing it fully... knowing that it is just an emotion and that you are so much more than any emotion...

3. Drop Down Through the experience.

This may feel strange, but you do know what it feels like when you drop ... so feeling that   feeling   of *dropping*,   just   drop down through that experience until you drop down underneath that feeling...What feeling or emotion lies underneath that emotion? And now just   imagine dropping   down through that feeling [use the language and terms that the person gives you.] And what feeling comes to you as you imagine yourself dropping down through that one?

[Keep repeating this dropping-down through process until the person comes to "nothing..." That is, to no feelings ... to a void or emptiness.]

4. Confirm the Emptiness

Just experience that "nothingness" or "void" for a moment. Good. Now let that nothingness open up and imagine yourself dropping through and out the other side of the nothingness. What are you experiencing when you come out the other side of the nothingness? What or whom do you see?

[Repeat this several times ... to a second, third, or fourth resource state.]

5. Meta-State each problem state

Use each resource state to meta-state each problem state. And when you feel X about Y, how does that transform things? And when you even more fully feel X →what other transformations occur? Valid and solidify: just stay right here in this X resource and as you experience it fully, what happens to the first problem state (#1)? When you *feel this* (fire anchor for each resource) ... what else happens to those old problem states?

6. Test

Let's see what now happens when you try, and I want you to really try to see if you can get back the problem state that we started with. When you try to do that, what happens? Do you like this? Would you like to take this into your future? Into all of your tomorrows and into all your relationships?

Meta-Stating Troubling Emotions

1. **Identify an emotion that you have a problematic relationship with.**

Something you've tabooed, that you try to avoid feeling. (In this process I tend to ask "what's behind that emotion?". Oftentimes, the first emotion people bring up is not the emotion that's really the issue. It's the emotion behind it that is the problem. As an example, I've had someone in the training who easily expressed his anger and yet he mentioned this as a troubling emotion. When I asked him what's behind the anger, he teared up and it turned out it was sadness that he was really trying to get away from)

2. **Check your permission level by going inside and saying "I give myself permission to feel X emotion".**

Notice any objections that might arise.

3. **As you've heard your objections, now go inside and say "I give myself permission to feel X emotion because..."**

Examples: "I give myself permission to feel anger because it allows me to recognize things that violate my values and to take appropriate action early." "I give myself permission to feel the tender emotions because it makes me more fully human."

4. **Bring other meta-states to the emotion (acceptance, appreciation, confidence, playfulness, humor, etc.)**

Check to see what meta-states you can texture the emotions with to welcome it in even more. Access, amplify, and apply that state to the (previously troubling) emotion.

5. **Future pace**

As you have these new understandings and feelings about this emotion in the days, weeks and months to come, what difference does that make? Are there any objections to this? Do you want to keep this?

Detection and Analysis #6: Troubling Relationship With Concepts

Meta-Stating Troubling Concepts

1. Identify a concept that gives you problems.

What concept do you want to develop a better relationship with? What concept, understanding, or idea pushes your buttons? What do you put into the sentence stem, *"I have a problem with . . ."*?

Menu List: authority, dependency, women, intimacy, entitlement, freedom, morality, vulnerability, criticism, fairness, failure, etc. What comes to you when you finish the sentence stem, *"I can't stand . . ."*?

2. Ground the concept to some real world trigger.

What sets off this idea or concept? What triggers it? When does it happen? In what context? What event or events elicit this response in you? What are the sensory-components of the trigger, the see-hear-feel variables?

3. Enter and explore the matrix of frames about the concept.

What do you believe about X? [Use the basic meta-questions to explore the frames and frames-within-frame. Remember to always enter the person's matrix with respect and exploration, without judgment or advice.]

What does X mean to you? When you think about X, what thoughts-and-feelings come to mind? What do you expect? And what do you believe about that? [Track the layers]

4. Quality control the construct of the concept.

Do you need this concept as part of your matrix of frames? Does it enhance your life or empower you? Is the framing of this concept useful or limiting? Healing or toxic?

5. Design a new more enhancing set of frames.

Just for the fun of it, playfully imagine yourself getting to choose another frame or meaning, how would you like to classify it, label it, evaluate it, or frame it? If you could magically use new frames of meanings that would enhance your life, what would you use? How would you like to think about or feel about these actions? [Build a new layer of meanings with the meta-questions. Embrace the new concept as a more useful concept and begin to texture it with other ideas that make it more useful, productive, and empowering.]

Detection and Analysis #7: Limiting Use Of Semantic Space

Social Panorama For A Coaching Session

Accessing Your Social Panorama

1. **Think about a coaching situation where you weren't performing at your best.**

Perhaps you were feeling lost, disconnected from your client, you focus was too much on yourself. You may have felt insecure around your client.

2. **As you go think of this situation, notice where in your mental space did you place your client?**

Are they in front of you or behind you, to your side? How far or how close are they?   And are they in color or black-and-white?

3. **How does this relationship affect your coaching?**

Does this allow you to feel unconditional positive regard for your client? Are you able to separate responsibility to / for? Does it allow you to hold your client accountable? What do you believe about yourself and your client here? What is the quality of your relationship?

4. **Make necessary changes to the position of your client in your mental space.**

Where would you need to place your client? What would be a better position for them that would allow them to feel safe, for you to feel ruthless compassion for them? In order to keep them in that position, what resources do they need? What new beliefs and understandings about them or yourself do you need?

(When guiding this process, you may inquire about a situation where the coach feels they are in their best possible coaching state and   determine where they've placed their client in that situation.)

5. **Transferring resources**

Do you have this resource? When have you experienced this in a powerful way? Go there. And feel what this resource feels like. Make it as lively and powerful as possible.

Then, in your mind, give this resource to your client. You can do this through putting it in a balloon or bubble and letting travel to your client and imagine the balloon popping open. Or it could be a mist of color or a symbol.

Notice how this allows your client to move to the desired position. Are other resources needed? If so, repeat step 5.

6. Future pace

Imagine stepping into a coaching session over the coming days, weeks, months to come, and your client is in this new position, what difference will that make? And what will that open up for you? What will it be like to have this even when you are challenged in your coaching session?

Detection and Analysis #8: Lack Of Motivation And Decision

Intentionality

1. **Identify an activity that's important but that does not feel important.**

What are some of the tasks that you engage in as part of your everyday life, career, etc.? What do you need to do in order to succeed that you know is important but it does not feel important to you? What activity do you have good intentions to do, but suffer from ADD   (Attention Deficit Disorder) when it comes time to actually do it?

2. **Explore the importance of the activity.**

Why is that activity important to you? Is this activity important and significant? *How* is it significant? *Why* is it valuable? Why is it meaningful? In what way? What else is important about that? How many other answers can you identify about this activity?

3. **Continue the exploration up the meta-levels.**

This activity is important because of these things, and why is this important to you? What's important by having this? What important about that outcome? And what's even more important than that? And when you get that fully and completely and in just the way you want it, what's even more important?

[Continue this until you flush out and detect all of the higher values.]

4. Step into the highest intentional state.

That' must be important to you? [Yes.] So just welcome in the good feelings that these meanings and significances invite, and just be with those higher level feelings for a bit. Do you like that? [Yes.] Let those feelings grow and intensify as you recognize that this is your *highest Intentional Stance*, this is what you are all about . . . is not it? Close your eyes and be with your highest intention and let it fill every fiber of your being.

5. Link to the highest state to the primary context.

Now in just a moment, when you are ready, I want you to open your eyes and look at that event that you started with, the event that you know is important but didn't feel important and look at it with all of these higher intentions in mind. As you now take this highest   intention — *look at that event* and notice how it aligns your attentions so your attentions can   now do serve for your intention. With this in mind, will you now be able to focus and   concentrate? Imagine taking this intentional stance and moving out into tomorrow with them.

6.   Commission your executive mind to take ownership.

There's a part of your mind that makes decisions, will that highest executive part of your mind take full responsibility to access this intention of your big Why whenever you are engaged in this activity so you can see the world this way? Imagine using this as *the basis of your inner life,* your way of being in the world. Do you like that?

Would that make a difference? Would you be able to focus on this activity and complete it?

[Optional] ***Invite other resources.*** Would you like to bring any other resource to this intentional stance? Would playfulness enrich it? Persistent? Passion? Etc.

7.   Future Pace.

Will you take this into your future? Will it enhance your life and align your attentions to your highest intentions? Will you keep this?

Part VI Focus Points

* In relaying our experience through language, a lot of information gets lost through distortion, deletion and generalizations. As a coach we need to recover the lost information in order to get to where the change power is.

* When we simplify it, when we habituate generalizations and deletions, we create thinking styles. The distortions create cognitive distortions. This is how the NLP Meta-Model, Meta-Programs and Aaron Beck's cognitive distortions are related.

* The Meta-Model is used to recover lost information, the Meta-Programs and cognitive distortions are used to discover patterns.

* Having a thorough grasp of the processes that solve the most common limiting patterns will help you co-create the desired change.

Acknowledgements

There are quite a few beautiful souls who have helped me in my journey to become an expert coach and which eventually led me to write this book.

Thank you Tonja Koudijs and Wassili Zafiris, for giving me a fun, safe and inspirational platform at the NLP trainings. It has been a great start from which I built all my subsequent learnings from.

Michael Hall, your work is profound. I stand in awe of the contribution you have made to the field of NLP and coaching. Thank you for everything.

A very special thanks goes out to Michelle Duval, co-founder of the Meta-Coach System and founder of Fingerprint For Success. Michelle, you touched my heart back in 2005 when I took my coach training with you. You saw me when I was trying to hide and make it through a tough week. And then you continued to be a guiding light in my life, both personally and professionally. I will be forever grateful.

When I started my own business back in 2008 I made a lot of mistakes. And I hardly made any money. My grandmother loaned me $10,000 to stay afloat while I followed my dream.

Money that she saved up over a great many years. She developed Alzheimer disease and has since passed away. I miss her, but my memories of her will forever last.

Cor and mam. Your support and steadfast belief in me has pulled me through the most difficult times of my journey. Thank you so much. And mam, I don't know what I'd do without you. I love you to the stars and back.

Tante Nellie. Thank you for listening. L.Y.T.T.S.A.B.

Scott, I love you. Thank you for believing in me, always. I'm so glad you dropped your fish at Little Joe's.

My clients give me new insights every day and they help me improve upon my work so I can serve them and future clients even better. To everyone I've worked with and am working with: you rock. Thank you for allowing me into your lives and helping you be great at coaching.

And lastly, a huge thanks goes to Lene Fjellheim from CoachTeam As in Oslo, Norway. Lene, I would not be where I am today without you. You have a unique ability to celebrate others and to lift them up. That's what you have done for me. I count myself blessed to call you my colleague, but above all, my friend. Thank you from the bottom of my heart.

Work With Me

If you'd like to dive deeper into the Quantum Leap Coaching System and get to expert level faster, I'd love to help you. By far the quickest way to truly transform your coaching is by putting it to practice, getting high quality feedback, and getting out of your own way. I know that a lot of coaches – that used to be me, too! – have a preference for reflection. So we read another book, philosophize some more, or have an addiction for the next a-ha moment without having to take action on it.

Remember: Making mistakes says nothing about how good you are or who you are as a person. That just leads to procrastination. I invite you to have fun with the system and get curious when you find yourself stuck. You can always email me when you do, I'm happy to answer any questions you may have.

I don't know where you are in your journey to master coaching, but there are several ways in which I can help you reach your goals. You can find out more about that at https://www.thecoachmentor.org. If you prefer to talk about what I can do for you, you can schedule an appointment https://www.thecoachmentor.org/apply.

If you are interested in live trainings on the Quantum Leap Coach System, please contact my partner organization CoachTeam As (www.coachteam.no, info@coachteam.no)

Bibliography

Bandler, Richard; Grinder, John. *The Structure Of Magic, Volume 1: A book about language and therapy.* Science and Behavior Books.

Belnap, Barbara; Hall, L. Michael (2004-11-01). *The Sourcebook of Magic (Second Edition): A comprehensive guide to NLP change patterns.* Crown House Publishing.

Bodenhamer, Bob; Hall, L. Michael. *The User's Manual For The Brain, Volume I.* Crown House Publishing.

Derks, Lucas. *Social Panoramas: Changing the unconscious landscape with NLP and Psychotherapy.*

Dilts, Robert. (1991). *Tools for dreamers: Strategies of creativity and the structure of innovation.* Capitola, CA: Meta Publications.

Duval, Michelle; Hall, L. Michael. *Meta-Coaching Volume 1: Coaching change for higher levels of success and transformation.* Neuro-Semantic Publications

Gallwey, W. Timothy. (1974). *The Inner Game of Tennis.* NY: Random House.

Goodenough, Tim (2016-07-13). *Game Changer Protocol: Free yourself from limiting beliefs and supercharge your life.*

Hall, L. Michael. *The Sourcebook of Magic II.* Washington D.C.: Library of Congress

Hall, L. Michael. (2003). *The Matrix Model.* Clifton, CO: Neuro-Semantic Publications.

Hall, L. Michael. (2011). *Benchmarking Intangibles: The Art of Measuring Quality.* Washington D.C.: Library of Congress

Hall, L. Michael; Bodenhamer, Bob. *The User's Manual For the Brain – Volume II*

Horsley, Kevin (2014-01-26). *Unlimited Memory: How to Use Advanced Learning Strategies to Learn Faster, Remember More and be More Productive.* TCK Publishing.

Linder-Pelz, Susie (2010-02-03). *NLP Coaching: An Evidence-Based Approach for Coaches, Leaders and Individuals.* Kogan Page.

Levitin, Daniel J. (2014-08-19). *The Organized Mind: Thinking Straight in the Age of Information Overload.* Penguin Publishing Group.

Printed in Great Britain
by Amazon

46738757R00155